P9-AQL-002

IN THE BEGINNING

by the same author

★

THE GREEKS AND THEIR GODS

THE GREEK PHILOSOPHERS
FROM THALES TO ARISTOTLE

ORPHEUS AND GREEK RELIGION:
A STUDY OF THE ORPHIC MOVEMENT

IN THE BEGINNING

*Some Greek views
on the origins of life and
the early state of man*

W. K. C. GUTHRIE

*Professor of Ancient Philosophy and
Master of Downing College, Cambridge*

METHUEN & CO LTD
36 ESSEX STREET · LONDON WC2

First published in 1957
Printed in Great Britain by
Western Printing Services Ltd
Bristol

CATALOGUE NO. 6015/U

'It is not wise, or even genuinely scientific, to brush aside as idle fancy or outworn superstition the experience of the greatest poets.'

F. M. CORNFORD

Contents

Preface

THIS book represents a series of Messenger Lectures at Cornell University, the purpose of which is stated in a note printed at the end. The foundation is not primarily a classical one. Indeed this is the first time in thirty-five years that the lectures have been allotted to the Classical Department, and it was impressed on the lecturer that they should be suitable for a general audience. At the same time the addition of notes will, it is hoped, give the work a certain interest for the classical student and scholar. They contain not only references to passages supporting the text, but also supplementary references and quotations, expansion of points which could only be summarily mentioned in the lectures, and a certain amount of additional information. Inevitably, however, the occasion of the work has imposed severe limitations.

Since preparing and delivering the lectures, I have seen a proof copy of Professor E. A. Havelock's book *The Liberal Temper in Greek Politics*, parts of which treat of much the same evidence as is here discussed, but from an entirely different point of view. As his title indicates, he is more interested in evaluating the political implications of certain early Greek scientific theories which I have preferred to treat in some detail for their own sakes. In particular, we differ *toto caelo* in our interpretations of the Protagoras myth. I see no reason to alter what I have written, but any reader of this book should be referred to his also (and perhaps *vice versa*).

The book is offered to my friends at Cornell in return for great kindness and a store of pleasant memories. Many have contributed to these, but I should like to say a special word of thanks to Fritz and Liselotte Solmsen and to our hosts at Telluride House. It was perhaps appropriate that these lectures should have been delivered within sight of Lake Cayuga in the Finger Lakes

[9]

country, the land of the Five Tribes who were united by the oratory of Hiawatha; for they too, like the Sown Men of Thebes, had once sprung up as a crop from the ground. We are told that Owayneo, the Great Spirit, took five handfuls of corn and dropped them, one in the valley of the Mohawk, one among the Flat Stones (or Oneida), one among the hills (Onondaga are the People of the Hills), one around Lake Cayuga, and the last around Lake Seneca; and from these grew the five great tribes.

The translation of the Horace ode by A. E. Housman on page 64 is included by permission of the Society of Authors and Messrs. Jonathan Cape Ltd.

W. K. C. G.

Melbourne, Australia,
July, 1957

I

Mother Earth

I. THE MYTHS

The woman in her conception and generation is but the
imitation of the earth, and not the earth of the woman.

PLATO, *Menexenus* 238a (trans. Jowett)

We are not so sentimental about the ancient Greeks today
as were our grandfathers in the 19th century. We have
a less idealized picture of them. This is not simply due
to the advancement of objective historical research, making possible a more accurate knowledge of their life and thought as it
actually was. The faults were known, and those who cared to do
so were perfectly well able to point them out. It is rather, I think,
that every age tends to bring into prominence those features of the
past which chime in best with its own ideas and preoccupations.
The heyday of classical studies was also a time of general optimism.
In England, most of those who taught and wrote about ancient
Greek civilization were products of the public-school system as
Thomas Arnold had reformed it, and of universities of which the
Oxford of Benjamin Jowett provides the most characteristic
example. They believed in that educational system as the one
which had formed our country for greatness and produced all the
best qualities in the British character. Since the classics played so
large a part in it, and the intrinsic greatness of much Greek and
Roman literature deservedly called forth their unstinted admiration
as it still does that of many of us today, there was a natural tendency

to look upon the Greeks and Romans as embodying the ancient counterparts of our own ideals. *Mens sana in corpore sano*, the phrase so insistently quoted in that period as summing up the essentials of the good life, was taken from the Roman poet Juvenal; and educators seized eagerly on anything which might go to show that the Greeks were not only the wisest of men but combined their wisdom with a proper admiration of athletic prowess and the glory of the perfect human body.

Today we are not so confident. Much has happened to make us more doubtful about the rightness of our ways and the nature of the goal which lies ahead of us. We see the symptoms of disease in our civilization, especially in the sphere of international relations and the destructiveness of war, and when we turn to the past it is with different questions in our minds. We try to look more realistically and to probe the faults of other ages, in the hope, consciously or unconsciously held, that this will help us to detect what is wrong in our own society and so, by putting it right before it is too late, to avoid the fate which has overtaken the often short-lived periods of high achievement in the past. Not only historical studies, but science and philosophy, come under the subtle influence of the spirit of the age. The ruling concept of Victorian science was biological evolution, and in philosophy one still saw the creation of bold and all-embracing metaphysical systems. The characteristic science of our own age is the introspective one of analytical psychology, and in philosophy we have seen the dethronement of metaphysics in favour of linguistic analysis. Some historians even seem to have given up the study of history, and study their fellow-historians instead, or historiography as they call it. We look at our own habits of thought and speech rather than at the external world about us. So in historical study, whereas every age is liable to project its own mind unconsciously into the past, it has been left for us to look consciously and anxiously for analogies to our present situation.

One result of this has been to bring the Greeks down from the pedestal on which our fathers had set them. They are seen less as the embodiment of wisdom and beauty, and more as ordinary human beings with quirks and foibles like the rest of us. Since this is certainly what they were, one cannot regret the change, and if we talk less today in terms of 'the Glory that was Greece , it nevertheless remains true that no one who has come into first-hand contact with their literature, philosophy or art can fail to be impressed and enlightened by the genuine greatness which they display. The Greeks can stand a closer inspection, and it is not necessary to cherish illusions in order to be convinced that the study of them is still worth while.

I want to suggest one reason out of many why this is so, to point to one aspect of the study of ancient Greece which among others ensures its perennial value; and then to introduce my subject as a particular illustration of what I have said. Later on, we shall find ourselves involved in a considerable amount of detail, and the inquiry will gain in interest if we have put it first of all in a wider setting and so can see it in the light of a larger idea. With this idea in mind from the start, we may follow Socrates's advice to let the argument blow us wherever it will, confident that, like Theseus in the labyrinth, we have a thread in our hands that will save us from getting lost.

What I have in mind is the comparatively small size of the Greek world and the rapidity with which its civilization developed. A modern historian once remarked to me that the historians of the late 19th century who had done most to turn their subject from a bare recital of facts to a deeper concern with the nature of historical processes were those who had been trained up in the classical field. It was this classical training that had enabled them to prophesy, in an era of superficial stability and progress, the coming of an age of great wars, revolutions, and popular military dictatorships. The reason was that the Greek city-state, with which they were first made familiar, was in physical size a small and convenient unit for study, and its history could be observed as an isolated phenomenon passing in the course of a few centuries through all political and social phases: monarchy, aristocracy, oligarchy and democracy. One could then follow the decline of democracy into chaos and the rise of the great empires within which the city-state finally lost its reality. Greece in short offered a microcosm, a small-scale working model of human society in all its phases.

[13]

My theme lies in the field, not of social or political history, but rather in that of the history of ideas. But here too the Greeks provide an analogous situation. In their outlook on the world of nature, its origins and the processes by which it is maintained, a predominantly rational and scientific temper made its appearance among them soon after 600 B.C. with a suddenness which has never ceased to cause astonishment; and this movement of natural philosophy reached its culmination in Aristotle less than 300 years later. I do not mean to ignore, as has sometimes been done in the past, the genuine achievements of the Hellenistic age which followed, particularly in the field of factual sciences like geography, of applied science and technology, and of mathematics. It was after all a Hellenistic engineer, Hero of Alexandria, who built the first known machine to illustrate the principle of jet propulsion.[1] Up to Aristotle Greek thought had a more speculative character; it was less interested in technical progress and more in the general principles underlying the workings of the universe at large, although the foundations of research in the special sciences, particularly biology, were of course laid by the enormous industry of Aristotle himself. Its object was simply to understand nature, not to dominate her, and it relied on a combination of observation and inference for the most part unsupported by controlled experiment. After Aristotle the particular urge towards knowledge for its own sake, which had started among the 6th-century Ionians, seems to fade out. Philosophers directed their energies rather to the construction of ethical systems within which a man could find comfort and guidance in the unpredictable and bewildering circumstances of the Hellenistic world, and what they said about the nature and government of the physical universe was subordinate to this aim. The spirit of free and independent intellectual inquiry flagged, and indisputably its last and greatest representative in the ancient world is Aristotle.

When we reflect that from the first beginnings of philosophy among the Greeks to the death of Aristotle in 323 B.C., little more than 250 years had passed, it is obvious that their mental development was exceptionally rapid. To study it is almost like watching a nature-film in which the growth of a plant from seed to flower has been so speeded up as to take place before the eyes in a matter of minutes instead of months. The development in question is from a mythical to a rational view of the world. Before the birth of philosophy, the Greeks, like other peoples at a similar stage of development, saw in natural phenomena the operations of benignant or angry deities. Thunder and lightning were the weapons of Zeus, storms and earthquakes the work of Poseidon. When Hesiod describes the origins of the world, he posits certain powers as present in the beginning and derives others from them. These powers are at one and the same time persons and parts or phenomena of the natural world—Earth and Sky, Night and Day—and because of their personal character the evolution of the universe can be unfolded in simple terms of human marriages and births. All that is needed is the god of love or desire (who was one of those existing from the beginning) and the process can carry on happily. Sky weds Earth. She bears the mountains and the ocean as her children in just the same way as she bears certain giants and gods whose form and function are purely anthropomorphic.

Philosophy is born when rational curiosity gets the upper hand, and rejecting the action of personal agents, men begin to seek the explanation of phenomena in the working-out of impersonal forces. The caprice of individual gods gives way to the search for general laws. In Greece mythological and religious explanations were unchallenged until about 600 B.C., yet by the middle of the 4th century Aristotle, with Plato behind him, could move as easily as we do ourselves in the field of abstract conceptions and universal principles.

Before this could happen a great deal of hard thinking and reasoned argument had had to take place. But the point is this. There is no sudden transition from a mythical to a rational mentality. Mythical thinking does not die a sudden death, if indeed it ever dies at all. One has only to consider that Aristotle himself, the founder both of biological science and of formal logic, believed to the end of his days that the stars were living and divine. We smile at this, but I suspect nevertheless that certain vestiges of the mythological mode of thought still lurk unrecognized in our own minds. We have given up the language of mythology and overlaid them with the terminology of reason, but that perhaps only makes them more dangerous. Are we not still tempted to personify Nature, matching Aristotle's statement that she 'makes nothing in vain' with such pronouncements as 'Nature abhors a vacuum', or endowing her (for we usually employ the feminine pronoun) with human characteristics, calling her according to our mood a kindly nursing mother or a cruel stepmother? Yet we should be puzzled to explain in what sense any single entity exists, whether personal or not, to which (or whom) the word 'nature' can properly be applied.[2]

In medicine we speak of diseases as entities which act in certain ways, yet it has been justly said that a doctor meets no diseases, only sick people, no two of whom have precisely the same symptoms. The broad classification of these symptoms is convenient, indeed for the progress of medical science it is necessary, but the attitude of mind which goes with it, the endowment of diseases with a substantial existence, may lead to a rigidity in practice which will be the reverse of beneficial to a patient. Is this mythology? Well, a distinguished physiologist has expressed the view that the conception of a disease as a substantial essence with an existence independent of the patient is an unconscious survival from the time when it was imagined as an evil spirit entering the body with malevolent intent.[3]

History and politics have their unconscious personifications too. Professor Butterfield has drawn attention to the fallacy of imagining, for example, the French Revolution as a 'thing', still worse as a self-acting agent that 'stood up and did something'. What happened was that a certain man or group of men took a decision or acted in a certain way. Today we hear on every hand of economic factors, wars, political situations as causing or doing certain things, whereas, he points out, they do not even exist except as abstract terms.[4]

In Greece too one can find the concepts of myth dressed up in rational terms and living on in the guise of philosophic ideas. But because the Greeks were much nearer than we are to the mythical or magical origins of their thought, these origins show through more clearly. To observe the gradual course of their intellectual

[16]

emancipation is in itself a fascinating pursuit—for we are looking at the development of the European mind in one of its most interesting and exciting phases—and may incidentally prove salutary by throwing an indirect light on the dubious credentials of some of the concepts that pass for rational and sensible today. If that happens, it will only be a by-product of our present investigation; but it is worth bearing in mind. In any case I want to look at my subject—the beginnings of life—as an instance of the remarkable way in which Greek thought provides a bridge between the worlds of myth and reason.

Let me take an example which is not too far from my chosen theme. Thales of Miletus in Ionia has been universally acclaimed as the first European to take the decisive step from myth to philosophy. His reputation rests on the pronouncement, attributed to him by Aristotle, that the world is fundamentally of one substance, and that substance is water. Now it is possible to see this as the outcome of a purely scientific combination of observation and rational thought. Historians of science point admiringly to the facts that a large part of the earth's surface is water, that the greater part of our bodies consists of nothing else and that life is impossible without it, that only water manifests itself in nature in the three forms liquid, solid and gaseous, and so forth. More than that. It is said that his actual choice of a basic substance is of secondary importance; his claim to be called the father of science is justified not so much by the answer he gave as by the actual question he asked. To inquire into the one thing at the basis of all nature, to try to explain the variety of the natural world as due to the modifications of something *within* it—this was the great triumph of human reason over the age-old superstition which saw in everything the caprice of supernatural beings. At last someone is dealing with true causes, things whose existence can be verified by observation. [5]

All this is true, but the story has another side as well. Can it be mere coincidence that Thales's native city Miletus was a thriving commercial port of the Levant, in close touch during his lifetime with Egypt, Babylonia and other ancient seats of civilization where a belief in the origin of the world from water had been held from time immemorial? The Egyptians owed their lives to the annual flooding of the Nile, and the Mesopotamian civilizations, as their name suggests, were no less intimately connected with the great river-systems that had given them birth. To the Egyptians, in consequence, the earth itself once arose out of Nūn, the primordial waters which, as also in Hebrew story, are still all around it, above as well as below and on its surface. In particular, they are the origin of all life and fertility, and on the first mud-hillock to appear above them the creator-god took his station. When we look back from a modern standpoint, it seems most likely that Thales got his idea from observing the transformations of water into solid ice and vapour, but that was not the opinion of Aristotle his fellow-Greek. For him the most probable connexion in Thales's mind was that between water and life. He remarks that vital heat is always accompanied by dampness, that all nourishment contains moisture and the life-creating sperm is also liquid. This seems to bring Thales even closer to ancient Egyptian ideas. When we turn to the Babylonian epic of creation, which goes back to nearly 2000 B.C., we find a similar picture of the primacy of water: the earliest stage of things was one of watery chaos. Even in Greek myth, Homer preserves traces of an old belief that Okeanos and Tethys, deities of water, were the original begetters of everything. As for the Hebrews, one writer has gone so far as to call the water of Thales simply 'the primordial mist familiar to us in the Biblical Garden of Eden story', a view which certainly takes us to the opposite extreme from those who uphold the original scientific insight of the Greek.[6]

What of his more fundamental concept, that the world has its origin in a single substance, to the modification of which its variety is to be attributed? This seems, in face of the multiplicity of phenomena, to be a remarkable feat of speculative reason. Yet at least we must say this: both in Greece and in the Near East generally it was an ancient and widespread belief that in the beginning all things were fused together in an undifferentiated mass. The initial act in the making of the world was regularly seen as the separation or division of what had been one. 'God *divided* the light from the darkness' said the Hebrew, 'and divided the waters which were under the firmament from the waters which were above the firmament'. In Greek mythology we find the re-current idea that in the beginning Heaven and Earth were 'one form'. Before anything else could happen, they had to be separated. Then they mated in human fashion, and Earth gave birth to the rest of nature. In general, the idea which the Greeks of later days attributed to their legendary poets Orpheus and Musaeus, that 'everything comes into being from one thing, and dissolves again into the same', was certainly current coin by the 6th century.[7]

In what I have just said I have made passing mention of the origin of life, and so of the particular topic of these lectures. The mystery of life is always with us, and although we now know far more about its earliest and most elementary forms, we cannot be said to have solved the problem of its first emergence from the non-living, or of the precise difference between the two. Naturally enough, few subjects have more keenly or constantly whetted the human appetite for knowledge, and the speculations of the Greeks upon it form one of the most curious and fascinating chapters in the history of their thought. Moreover they illustrate especially clearly how slow and difficult, even among a people of the liveliest intellect, is the transition from the mythical to the rational view-point, and how persistent the effect of one upon the other. To see them in this light will, I hope, give to our inquiry both an inner coherence and a relevance to the wider history of ideas; for as I have briefly tried to show, the power of myth to determine uncon-sciously the forms later assumed by philosophical or scientific systems is not confined to Greece or to the past.

It will now be obvious that, at least in so far as their mythology was real for them, the realm of life extended more widely for the Greeks than it does for us, and the line between animate and inanimate was less sharply drawn. It is true—and if true, of the highest importance—that for the modern scientist, as in the Greek world for Aristotle, such a line may be difficult to detect or even non-existent. Sir Charles Sherrington went so far as to write:[8]

Aristotle noted of life that its lower limit defies demarcation. The living and the non-living, he thought, merge one in the other gradually. Today the very distinction between them is convention. This deletes 'life' as a scientific category; or, if you will, carries it down to embrace the atom. The vanishing point of life is lost.

At the moment however I am not thinking of the findings of modern science so much as of the language of ordinary experience. Normally we make the distinction, and to us the earth, for example, is not alive. We are still very conscious that it produces the grains, fruits and vegetables by which we live. If we eat meat, we still subsist on its bounty at one remove, for our cattle have been pastured on the grass of the fields. To express this indebtedness we often speak of Mother Earth, but we are well aware that this is metaphorical language. For the Greeks on the other hand, as for many other peoples, the worship of the earth as the Great Mother was one of the oldest forms of their religion, if not the oldest of all. It was established in the lands around the Aegean Sea long before invaders brought with them the idea of a male father-god as the supreme deity, and instead of supplanting her, the patriarchal Zeus and his brothers soon found themselves compelled to come to terms. The veneration of the earth-goddess persisted—or, one might say, of the earth-goddesses. The plural is easily explained. The Earth-mother was a deity very close to her worshippers and to the soil from which they got their livelihood. Naturally therefore, especially in early days when communities were small and isolated, she had many names in different places, and the Mother of one district might even be a rival of her counterpart in another. Nevertheless I think that when contact was made through travel, war or commerce, all were conscious that she was everywhere the same spirit, the spirit of the life-giving earth, manifested in its fruits and all its creatures. We need not demand logic from the feelings of simple peasants. The same attitude persists today, for in Mediterranean lands the Virgin of one village may be seen in rivalry with the Virgin of another, although intellectually all would admit that there can be only one Mother of Christ. We have real continuity of tradition here, for in many places the Virgin has succeeded to the pagan cult of the Great Mother. She too had her

Son, and in the pre-Christian history of this pair lies some of the explanation why, in the lands where she once was supreme, the Virgin Mary sometimes means more to simple Christians than does her divine Son himself.

All this can be read of elsewhere. I mention it only to make the point that in Greek religion the Earth was one of the oldest of the gods. In the earliest Greek poetry she is invoked along with Zeus, the Sun and the Furies to call down curses on the oath-breaker, and we have seen how she appears in Hesiod as one of the first of divine beings and the ancestor of those who came after. How literally, and in what exact sense, the Greeks interpreted the appellation 'Mother of all', by which they referred to her, we shall see shortly.[9]

Most people know the story of Cadmus. Destined to found the city of Thebes, he discovered the site by following a cow which the gods had sent to guide him. Before he could draw water from the neighbouring spring, he had to kill the dreadful serpent which guarded it, and on the advice of Athena sowed its teeth in the ground, from which sprang a crop of armed men. Euripides tells the tale in full, and Ovid describes with a somewhat ludicrous precision the emergence of this unusual crop.[10] Obedient to the goddess, Cadmus ploughed a furrow and scattered the teeth in it.

> Then—a wonder beyond belief—the clods began to move, and the tip of a spear appeared above the ground. Soon helmets emerge, nodding with painted crests, then shoulders, chests, arms grasping weapons, and so there grows the harvest of shield-bearing warriors.

Five of them survived the battle which followed. The names of four—Echion, Pelor, Oudaios and Chthonios—are clear evidence of their origin, for they mean Snake-man, Monster, Man of the Ground and Man of the Earth. Since snakes were always closely associated in cult with the earth, and earth-born heroes identified with snakes, all four names point in the same direction. The serpent from whose teeth the warriors sprang is itself called 'earth-born' by Euripides. These four with their fellow-survivor Hyperenor

('Overweening') became the ancestors of the Thebans, who were in consequence known as Spartoi, 'the sown men'.[11]

Practically the same story is told of Jason, who before he could win the Golden Fleece was compelled by King Aeetes to yoke a pair of fire-breathing bulls, plough a stretch of land, and sow some of the remaining teeth of the serpent slain by Cadmus. Once again there sprang up a crop of 'earth-born men'.

I have purposely started from the fairy-tale end, choosing stories that are widely known outside the field of scholarship, if only from their retelling by Charles Kingsley in *The Heroes*. It seems natural to look upon them as stories pure and simple, with no bearing on any theories of the origins of life that were ever seriously held. But we shall see. We may start by setting in a wider reference the Greek word *gēgenēs*, meaning 'born from the earth', which is appropriately applied in these stories to the men who emerged from the soil like a crop of wheat. 'The earth-born crop of sown men', Euripides calls them, and in applying the same epithet to the serpent he emphasizes its kinship with them as a child of earth.[12] The epithet was also applied to another mythical race, the race of giants, both collectively and individually. In the far-off days before Zeus was established in his present position of lordship over gods and men, Earth bore these huge and violent creatures to her husband Ouranos ('Heaven'), and a great battle had to be fought with them before the power of Zeus and the other gods could be secure. They were often thought of simply as an earlier generation of men, larger, fiercer and more uncouth than the present one. Hesiod tells of their birth, and later poets give them this epithet of *gēgenēs*.[13]

Certain legendary heroes, especially those whom living Greek tribes or peoples claimed as their first ancestors, contain the word 'earth' in their names or are associated with it in other unmistakable ways. The Greeks believed that the earliest inhabitants of their country were called Pelasgi, from a common ancestor Pelasgos. The Arcadians in particular laid claim to him, and Pausanias writing on Arcadia quotes two lines from an ancient poet Asius which say: 'The black earth brought him forth, that the race of mortals might be.' Hesiod also, we are told, said that he sprang

from the soil. In another story he was king of Argos and had a
human father, but this father had himself a transparent name,
Palaichthon, the two components of which mean 'long ago' and
'earth'. Not surprisingly, Aeschylus gives to him too the epithet
gēgenēs. In Attica the common ancestor was Erechtheus, of whom
Homer says that 'the grain-bearing ploughland gave him birth',
and Herodotus duly calls him *gēgenēs*. Athena, goddess of Athens,
was his nurse, and at the end he was taken back alive by the earth,
which, struck by the trident of Poseidon, opened and swallowed
him. He was worshipped with Athena in a joint temple on their
own Acropolis, where once stood the palace from which he
ruled. His name contains the root of *chthon*, earth, and originally
he was probably identical with Erichthonios, who was also
gēgenēs and had Athena for his nurse. She entrusted a chest in
which he lay to the daughters of Cecrops, with instructions not to
open it; but curiosity overcame them, and the story went that what
they saw inside was a serpent or serpents. Cecrops himself was in
classical times generally regarded as the first king of Athens,
having probably supplanted Erechtheus in the popular mind,
and his origin is indicated by his representation as half-man, half-
snake. So we see him in art, and Euripides speaks of his twisting
coils.[14]

The possession of an ancestor who was in this literal sense a
child of earth went with the claim of the peoples themselves to
belong to the land on which they lived. They were *autochthones*—
autochthonous as we now say, unless we translate it by words like
'aboriginal' or 'native'. Often it seems to mean no more, as when
Herodotus says that the Carians rejected the Cretan story that they
had migrated to the mainland of Asia Minor from the islands in
favour of their own claim that they were autochthonous. Above
all other Greeks the Athenians boasted of this distinction. Attica
belonged to them because they alone of the Greeks were no immi-
grants or invaders, but the original sons of the country. So also we
might speak today, but to a Greek the word *autochthones* meant
more. Plato shows that its original meaning survived when he
applies it to the giants. So does Isocrates, who more than once
employs it to enhance the glory of the Athenian people.

[23]

'We hold our land,' he says in the *Panegyricus*, 'not by right of having expelled others, nor by coming upon it uninhabited, nor yet by being gathered into it as a mixture of many races. No, our birth is so fine and pure that we have from all time continued in the very land *from which we sprang*. We are *autochthones*, and can address our city by the same names as our nearest kin. Alone of the Greeks we can call her not only native land but mother and nurse.'

Our modern race-fanatics must envy a credulity which could lend such infallible support to their pretensions.[15]

In token that they had sprung from the soil, the older men of Athens had a custom, already obsolete in the time of Thucydides and Aristophanes, of wearing in their hair gold ornaments in the shape of cicadas; for the cicada too was believed to be in some strange way generated from the earth.[16]

In dealing with the myths of Greece, one must resist the temptation to impose a non-existent unity or consistency. The Hebrews knew of only one first man, Adam, created by God from the dust of the ground. Among the Greeks we find a very different state of affairs, due partly to their fertile and irrepressible imagination, but more to the fact that they were always divided into a number of small and highly competitive tribal or political units, each of which felt bound to put in its claim to be the oldest, and to possess its land by a better right than the others. Either therefore each put forward a different ancestral hero, or if one myth became particularly dominant and widespread, each must try to annex it, with the result that the same hero appears to have been born in a surprising number of places. The earth-born Pelasgos belonged particularly to Arcadia, whose inhabitants claimed that he sprang from their soil. But as the Pelasgi came to be regarded as the forerunners of the Greeks in general, so we find him turning up as the ancestor—still autochthonous—of other communities in different parts of the country. Deucalion was another from whom all the present generation were supposed to be descended, because he and his sister Pyrrha were the only survivors of the Flood. Accordingly we find that their landing took place in a bewildering variety of localities—on Mount Parnassus near Delphi, Mount Othrys in Thessaly, even Mount Aetna in Sicily and elsewhere. The Ararats of Greece were many. Aristotle says that the Flood took place particularly in what he calls old Greece, meaning, as he says, the home of the oldest Greek peoples. This he thinks is the country round Dodona in the West, but his words explain why the story was attached to other places too: the title of 'the oldest of the Greek peoples' was coveted by all the quarrelsome Greek communities alike.[17]

I mention this irreducible variety because at this point the question might suggest itself: did the Greeks believe that *all* men were descended from earth-born ancestors, or only certain peoples? When the Athenians claimed sole right to the title *autochthones*, the thought at the back of their minds was that they were the oldest race and their first ancestor was the ancestor of all mankind. In Plato's dialogue *Menexenus* Socrates recites a speech in praise of Athens which is, as he admits, a cento of contemporary commonplaces, and in it he says:

> At the time when the whole earth was sending up and bringing to birth creatures of every kind, both animals and plants, our own land was innocent and barren of wild beasts: she made her own choice and brought forth man, the superior of the animals in intelligence and the only respecter of morality and religion.

As proof of this the writer goes on to make another familiar claim, that only in Attica did the earth produce grain, the staff of human life, which other peoples possess by the generosity of the Athenians; and it is natural that, as with a woman, the same land should be both mother and nurturer of her offspring. 'For,' he adds (and it is a remark highly significant for this whole climate of belief), 'in her pregnancy and childbirth it is a woman who imitates the earth, and not the other way round'.[18]

In truth however the makers and first propagators of these myths were hardly thinking in universal terms. The tendency to do so increased with the growth of civilization and rational thought, and the idea that all mankind everywhere may have originated from within the earth meets us most frequently in Plato and Aristotle. But we do not find anything like a consistent evolution of ideas. Even for Aristotle the Flood was a local Greek affair, whereas in Ovid as in the book of Genesis it is the whole race of men whom Zeus wipes out for their wickedness, and the waters extended over the whole earth. This does not necessarily mean that Ovid drew on a later source. Amid all the conflicting local claims the belief was current quite early that human life did not begin in Greece at all, but in Egypt. Herodotus discusses this quite seriously, and Aristotle speaks of the Egyptians 'whom we hold to be the most ancient of mankind'.[19]

Before we finally leave the story of Deucalion, it is interesting to notice how two different motives are conflated within it. These are, first, the story of the ultimate origin of mankind, which commonly describes them as in one way or another produced from the earth; and secondly, the story of a universal catastrophe leaving only one, or at most a handful of human survivors, who in consequence are the common ancestors of all now living. Such catastrophes, as we shall see from Plato and Aristotle, were often believed to recur at regular intervals, and the two types of story have behind them two different views about the origins of the world as a whole. According to one belief, our world had a beginning in time. From primal chaos a cosmos is formed in due succession. First earth and sky are separated, then earth brings forth plants, then animals, and finally men. According to the other, the world has existed from all time, and is subject not to a continuous development but to a cyclic alternation. Periodically a cataclysm occurs, which without destroying the main fabric of the cosmos, nevertheless wipes out all civilization and compels the survivors to start life again from the most humble and rudimentary beginnings.

It is of course this second type that is illustrated by the myth of the Flood. But the story of Deucalion continues thus. When the waters had subsided and Deucalion and Pyrrha prayed to the gods for companions, they were told (either by Zeus through Hermes or by Themis) to throw stones behind their backs, and these stones became men and women. Why stones? The version known to Ovid gives the answer. It says that the instruction was given in oracular form, for what they were in fact commanded to throw behind them was 'the bones of their mother'. Pyrrha was shocked, but Deucalion saw what was meant, and explained to her that their mother was the earth, and the bones in her body were the stones. To recreate the race of men, recourse must once again be had to her from whom they had their first beginning.[20]

We have been looking at stories in which the first men sprang naturally, like plants, or at least automatically, from the earth—though not indeed without divine intention. There are others in which a god or gods acted directly, modelling men out of mud or clay with their own hands. The best-known nowadays is that of Prometheus, though it is noteworthy that in the earliest versions of his story he appears only as man's benefactor and civilizer, not as his creator. Even in the impressive recital of his services to man, in the great play of Aeschylus of which he is the hero, he makes no mention of this supreme achievement, and Hesiod also is silent about it. Classical literature does give us references to mankind as 'creatures moulded of clay', and these may well be allusions to Prometheus, whose part in things is thus described by Ovid:

As yet there lacked a living creature more divine than the beasts, to rule the rest of nature. Then man was born, whether it be that the divine artificer created him from the seed of the gods or that the earth, fresh and lately sundered from the lofty ether, still retained some seeds of the kindred heaven, then Prometheus mixed it with rainwater and moulded it into the image of the gods who govern all.

Similarly Apollodorus in his comprehensive summary of Greek myths says briefly that Prometheus fashioned men out of earth and water. But Plato in the *Protagoras* speaks generally of 'the gods'. There the sceptical Sophist Protagoras, deliberately casting his account of life and society in the form of a myth, begins:

Once upon a time there existed gods but no mortal creatures. When the appointed time came for these also to be born, the

[27]

gods formed them within the earth out of a mixture of earth and fire and the substances which are compounded from earth and fire.

Prometheus comes into the story later, and as in the other tales, provides men with the technical skills necessary for survival.[21]

In this chapter our illustrations of the idea that men and animals could be born from the earth have been taken from the realm of myth, or as we might call it, fairy-tale. Yet we have seen evidence that such stories were taken seriously enough to be used by politicians and patriotic poets in the interests of propaganda. Perhaps it is some comfort to know that the absurdities alleged in the cause of rampant nationalism were as rife in the 5th century before Christ as they are today. At any rate, to see them in this (to us) plainly unacceptable form may put us on our guard against their modern counterparts: Nordic man, 'blood and soil', or the subtler temptation to personify the idea of a nation in a non-existent female figure. At the same time it would be unfair to suggest that the practical effect of the belief in autochthony was wholly bad, leading only to arrogance and aggression. One can well imagine the strength and courage that it gave the Athenians when they faced alone the Persian invaders of Greece. In future chapters we shall turn to some more scientific theories of the origin of life, supported by serious argument. It was no easy problem for the earliest philosophers. The usual processes of generation call for previously existing parents. How then was life given to the first creatures of all? As Lucretius pertinently remarked: 'Neither can living animals have fallen from the sky nor the beasts of earth have issued from the salt pools.' He himself adopted what was perhaps, in the absence of modern biological knowledge and a soundly-based theory of evolution, the only reasonable alternative: 'It remains that rightly has the earth won the name of mother, since out of earth all things are produced.' We shall see how the earth-born creatures fared in the transition from myth to reason.[22]

[28]

2

Mother Earth

II. THE SCIENTIFIC, APPROACH

Nam ut mittam quod fabulares poetarum historiae ferunt,
homines primos aut Promethei luto esse formatos aut Deuca-
lionis Pyrrhaeque duris lapidibus esse natos, quidam ex ipsis
sapientiae professoribus nescio an magis monstruosas, certe non
minus incredibiles rationum suarum proferunt rationes.

CENSORINUS, *De die natali* 4

In the last chapter we looked at some myths of the origin of
human life which obviously had more than a fairy-tale reality
for classical Greece. In later times there were Greek writers of a
more sceptical turn who were not slow to make fun of them.
Lucian in the 2nd century A.D. could laugh at the Athenians for
talking about Erichthonios as the child of Earth, and supposing
the first men to have grown out of the soil of Attica like vegetables;
though this, he adds, is at least a more respectable story than the
Theban one about sown men springing up from a serpent's teeth.
But, he goes on, we must not be too hard on them. After all, if the
Greeks were robbed of their myths, their professional guides would
starve, because this is the sort of thing that the tourist wants to
hear![1]
   I am not going to talk about the Greece of Lucian, already
living on her past as a playground for tourists from all parts of the
Roman Empire. My question is: what were the conclusions of
those who from the 6th century B.C. onwards, side by side with a

still living belief in the traditional mythology, tried to banish it from their minds and produce the first rational accounts of the origin of human life?

Before we approach them directly, there is something to be added to our account of the mythical background. In producing life as we actually observe it to do—that is, vegetable life—the earth needs to be fertilized by water, whether it come from the sky or from rivers. Since in most parts of Greece the only rivers are small torrents that dry up in summer, the main emphasis was on the rain, and in mythical terms the process was thought of as the mating of the male sky-god with his wife Earth. In Greece, the chief sky-god was the supreme deity Zeus, whose constant titles were Cloud-gatherer and Father, and there are many stories in which the partners in this 'sacred marriage' are named as Zeus on the one hand and one of the many local earth-goddesses on the other; but sometimes the meaning is made more transparent by calling the partners simply Earth and Heaven, though the language of love between the sexes is still retained. Aeschylus wrote:

> Love moves the pure Heaven to wed the earth; and love takes hold on Earth to join in marriage. And the rain, dropping from the husband Heaven, impregnates Earth, and she brings forth for men pasture for corn, the life of man,

and Euripides referred to Earth as the mother not only of plant but also of animal life in a choral invocation to

> Divine Aether, Father of men and gods, and Earth who receivest the moist drops of the showers and bearest mortals, bearest plants and the tribe of beasts; whence rightly thou art called Mother of all.

In this way the elements primarily involved in the generation of life were to the Greek mind earth and water: life sprang from a union or marriage of the dry with the liquid. Similarly in the stories of human beings being actually fashioned by the hand of a god, the material used is clay or mud. For the making of the woman Pandora, Zeus ordered Hephaestus to mix earth and water, and in Ovid's story Prometheus did the same. This tradiditional background must be borne in mind when we are considering the large part played by the interaction of the dry and moist elements in the theories of the philosophers. [2]

Of Thales, who in Aristotle's eyes was the first materialist philosopher, we really know very little for certain. Either he wrote nothing, or what he wrote was lost before the time of the first extant Greek authors who refer to him. Aristotle himself is dependent on hearsay and his own conjecture. Thales had however a younger friend and fellow-worker Anaximander, whose written works survived until Aristotle's time and beyond, and who therefore is the earliest Greek philosopher about whose description of the world and its origins we can begin to form some coherent idea. Like Thales, he too supposed the world to be derived from a kind of uniform mass, though not of wetness. He called it simply the Infinite or the Indefinite, because in the beginning none of the variously qualified substances that make up the present world had as yet any distinct character or existence of its own. Nothing as yet could be called wet or dry, hot or cold. This chaotic mass was, however, in everlasting and probably rotatory motion, which had a sifting effect; so it happened that at length, in a certain part of it, the variously constituted forms of matter began to be separated out. Here was the nucleus of a cosmos. The hot formed a sphere of flame enclosing colder material within it. Once started, the process continues from natural causes. Wet and dry are the next to separate, and they do so under the action of heat on a solid, damp mass. Thus the sphere is first filled with cloud or mist, and beneath it the great land and water masses of the earth begin to take shape. The pressure of the vapour eventually bursts the envelope of fire, which breaks up into the celestial bodies—sun, moon and stars.

We must resist the temptation to pursue these early cosmogonies into their fascinating detail, and concentrate on our main topic, the origin of life on earth. This according to Anaximander resulted from a natural continuance of the action of the hot and dry on the cold and moist. How it worked out we can gather only from tantalizingly brief statements by much later writers. Here they are.

Animals come into being from the moist in the course of its vaporization by the sun; and man originally resembled another creature, namely a fish.

In the beginning man was born from creatures of another species. This he inferred from the fact that other animals quickly find their own nourishment, whereas man alone needs a long period of nursing: hence he could not at first have survived as he now is.

Anaximander says that the first animals had their birth in the wet element. They were enclosed in spiny shells, and as they grew older came out on to dryer ground, where the shell split and they survived for a short time only.

Anaximander of Miletus gave it as his opinion that from water and earth when they had become heated there arose either fish or creatures resembling fish. Inside these grew human beings, the embryos being retained until puberty. Then they broke open and men and women emerged already able to feed themselves.

Anaximander affirmed, not that fish and men were of the same family, but that men at first were born and nurtured in fish. . . , and when they were capable of looking after themselves they emerged and took to the land.[3]

These statements may sound fantastic, but at least we cannot fail to be impressed by the complete change in language and outlook from the stories which we looked at in the last lecture. As St Augustine truly says, 'In these operations he attributes nothing to a divine mind'. If not science, at least the outlook and atmosphere of scientific thinking have come to birth. The surviving accounts are not altogether consistent. It would be surprising if they were, when we consider both the late date and the varied motives of the reporters. But on the balance of the evidence, Anaximander's reasoning seems to have been something like this. Life arose out of a combination of earth and water when they were heated to a certain temperature. It must therefore have started where the two elements were found together, as on the sea-bed or in rivers or pools. Hence the earliest living creatures are likely to have been aquatic. Man cannot have made his first appearance in the helpless form of a naked human baby, or he would have had no chance of survival. Doubtless then he was mothered by one of the aquatic creatures and not born into the world until already adult. If we accept an almost certain emendation of three words in the text of Plutarch which I omitted from the last of the passages just quoted, Anaximander adduced as a parallel a species of dogfish which was believed to have the peculiarity of extruding its young and taking them back into its body at will. In describing the appearance of these early foster-mothers of mankind, he seems to have had in mind the echinus or sea-urchin. [4]

It has sometimes been thought that Anaximander has here produced a theory of the evolution, on Darwinian lines, of man from a fishlike ancestor. But the theory I have just described is not this, and it sounds from most of the accounts as if he saw no reason to doubt that men appeared as early as any other form of life. His only proviso is that they cannot have been launched on the world as infants, and the theory is designed to show how the earliest men and women might have been protected till maturity. But if we cannot find the pure milk of Darwinism in the middle of the 6th century B.C. (we shall see something much closer to it in the 5th), we can yet spare a moment to admire the earliest effort to shake off the trammels of myth and put forward a theory on the sole basis of reason and a certain amount of observation, admitting none but purely natural causes.

At the same time, the pattern that he has adopted seems to echo unconsciously the mythology of his people. Everything starts from a single, heaving mass, in which there is no distinction to be perceived between earth and sky, land and water. Even so the myths said that in the beginning 'earth and sky were one form', and had to be separated before they could give birth to living things. 'Separating-out' (*ekkrisis*) was the keyword by which Anaximander accounted for the making of the world and all the creatures in it. He gives us first the 'separating-out' of the elements from each other, and later the 'separating-out' of life from earth and water, under the action of heat. Is it a coincidence that the first men had sometimes been thought of as the fruit of a mating between a river-

C

god and the earth? Is it a coincidence that in story the first woman
was created out of a mixture of earth and water, and moreover that
Hephaestus, god of fire, was the artificer? Prometheus was not a
very different figure, for it was he who brought the gift of fire to
men. Just why fire was so important in the scheme we may see
more fully in a later chapter, but for the moment we may remind
ourselves of the seriously-held belief that life arose spontaneously
from the wet mud of the Nile under the vivifying action of the sun.
This to Anaximander's contemporaries was no myth and must
have seemed strong confirmation of his theory, if indeed it was not
in part its cause.

When I ask if these correspondences can have been due to
simple coincidence, this is not a purely rhetorical question designed
to dismiss Anaximander as a mere rationalizer of myth with no
original contribution to offer. There is a real question here, which
is worth pondering. This becomes clear if it is transferred (as I
think it can be without absurdity) to a different age. Is it mere coincidence that the labours of men like A. R. Wallace and Charles
Darwin brought to its full flower the theory of the evolution of
species by natural selection at a time when the doctrine of laissez-
faire was yielding its richest harvest in the economic sphere, and
the climate of thought in England was pervaded by what we now
regard as the myth of an inevitable progress in human affairs? We
may perhaps answer, first, that it was probably not coincidence,
and secondly (what is indeed obvious) that this in no way detracts
from the permanent scientific value of what these men discovered.
The interests of a scientist or a philosopher are inevitably coloured
by the mental atmosphere in which he lives, and that, I suggest,
is why certain branches of science progress especially rapidly in
one particular age, and others in another. It is not far-fetched to
suppose that the prevailing tone of economic and social ideas in
mid-Victorian England, what one may with little exaggeration
call its mythology, encouraged Darwin and others towards the
idea of natural selection. From similar causes, perhaps, it was left
to a slightly later age and a different country to produce Sigmund
Freud and *his* discoveries, and their general acceptance and application came later still. Those who come after can take up into the

body of science all that is of permanent value. To link it with its own temporal background is not to diminish its validity; it only explains why one discovery rather than another was made just when it was.[5]

The general view of Anaximander that life arose in the moist element is attested in the next century for Anaxagoras and Democritus.[6] We may now consider a more detailed description of how it originated, one which has had a long history, for it may be traced, as a seriously-held theory, from the 5th century B.C. into Roman times, and passed from the Greek to the Moslem world, where it reappears in the 12th century A.D. It is particularly attributed in our sources to Epicurus and his school, but there are indications that it existed earlier, and this is inherently likely, since in physical matters Epicurus was largely content to reproduce the views of his predecessors. This account states that in the early days of the earth's existence, the action of warmth on mud produced growths which are compared to wombs and described as thin bubble-like membranes. Within these envelopes a kind of fermentation was continued by the sun's heat, and when finally the 'wombs' or envelopes burst, living creatures emerged from them. A curious corollary in some sources is that at the same time a milk-like liquid exuded from the earth, to provide the earliest nutriment for these human and animal infants.

The Roman encyclopaedist Censorinus ascribes the theory to Epicurus in this rather clumsily condensed form:

> He believed that when mud was heated, first of all there grew upon it a sort of wombs rooted in the earth. When these had brought forth infants, they produced from themselves a milk provided by nature, and the infants thus reared, when adult, propagated the human race.

The Epicurean version of Lucretius runs as follows:

> Then it was that the earth first gave birth to the race of animals. For much heat and moisture abounded then in the fields; thereby, whenever a suitable spot or place was afforded, there grew up wombs, clinging to the earth by their roots; and when

in the fullness of time the age of the little ones, fleeing moisture and eager for air, had opened them, nature would turn to that place the pores in the earth and constrain them to give forth from their opened veins a sap, most like to milk; even as now every woman, when she has brought forth, is filled with sweet milk, because all the current of her nourishment is turned towards her paps.

Lucretius's younger contemporary Diodorus reproduces a more circumstantial account in Greek:

When the earth was first separated from the fiery heaven in the universal whirl, it was 'clayey and altogether soft. As the sun's fire shone down on it, it solidified. Then by reason of the warmth its surface fermented [the word used applies literally to the leavening of bread with yeast], some of the wet parts swelled up in many places, and at those places there arose centres of putrefaction surrounded by thin membranes. This phenomenon may still be observed in marshes or stagnant pools, when the ground has cooled and the air is suddenly ignited owing to the rapidity of the change. While the moist patches were being impregnated with life by warmth in the way I have described, they received nourishment directly during the nights from the mist that fell from the surrounding atmosphere, and by day they were given solidity by the heat. Finally when the embryos had achieved their full development, and the membranes, being thoroughly heated, had burst, all kinds of animals were born. Those which had received the greatest portion of warmth became winged and took to the upper regions, those which retained an earthy composition made up the order of reptiles and other terrestrial animals, and those which had the largest amount of the moist element resorted to the appropriate habitat and are called aquatic. As for the earth, as it hardened further under the sun's fire and the winds it lost the power of producing the larger animals, and living creatures were henceforth engendered by copulation with each other.[7]

Other Greek versions which repeat the same language, and seem to go back to the same lost original, add one or two details, such as the comparison of the membranes to bubbles and the statement that male and female were distinguished by the amount of heat in their composition, males being hotter and 'better concocted' than females. The account as Diodorus gives it has got away as far as possible from the analogy of human motherhood, which was however never far from the surface. For instance, Diodorus gives a purely geological explanation of the fact that animals are no longer born from the earth: a certain admixture of moisture is necessary, and in the course of centuries the earth has hardened and dried out too much. But Lucretius openly adverts to the fact that in this the earth resembles a woman, who likewise can only bear children up to a certain age. We have an even more obvious analogy in the strange notion that the earth secreted a milk-like fluid for the nourishment of her own young.[8]

I have said that there are traces of this theory before the time of Epicurus. One thinks especially of Archelaus of Athens, a philosopher whose date in the middle of the 5th century B.C. is fixed by the tradition that he was a pupil of Anaxagoras and teacher of Socrates. Only short notes of his views have come down to us. In Diogenes Laertius we read:

> He says that the animals were born from the earth when it was warm, and it sent up an ooze resembling milk to serve as nourishment: it produced men in the same way.

Hippolytus puts it like this:

> Concerning animals he says that as the earth grew warm first of all in its lower part, where hot and cold were blended, many kinds of animals appeared including man. All had the same diet, being nurtured on the ooze, and they were short-lived. Later on they were engendered from each other.

This account so far as it goes is entirely consistent with the one which Epicurus adopted, and since Archelaus even supplied the notion of terrestrial milk, it seems likely that if we had further details of his views they also would correspond with our later accounts.[9]

It is also probable that these were the views of Democritus at about the same time. It is well known that Epicurus borrowed the atomic theory of matter from him and made it the basis of his own cosmology, and in introducing Epicurus's account of the origin of human life which has already been quoted, Censorinus brings the two into connexion with these words: 'Democritus of Abdera held that men were first created from water and mud. The view of Epicurus is similar, for he believed . . .'[10]

To illustrate the potent influence of the theory, we may step outside the Greek world for a moment to look at the version of the Andalusian Arab writer Ibn Tufayl (d. 1185). He relates that according to some authorities there is an island at the equator on which, because it possesses the most perfect and equable climate on earth, men are born without father or mother. A certain hollow on this island contains clay which in the course of centuries has fermented, owing to the particular proportions in it of the hot and the cold, the moist and the dry. The central portion presents the mixture most perfectly adapted to produce the seminal humours, and resembling most closely the composition of the human body. Being at the same time of a high viscosity, it gave rise to bubbles, one of which was divided into two by a thin membrane and filled with a subtle airy substance. In this appeared the soul, united so closely with the body as to be scarcely distinguished by the sense or understanding. There follows a great deal of detail about the formation of the embryo, after which it is said that the envelopes parted and the clay opened by reason of its increasing dryness, and thus the hero of this philosophical romance was born. There is however nothing here of any natural milk being provided by his mother the earth, for the author goes on to say that hunger caused the infant to cry, and he was suckled by a doe which had lost its fawn and was attracted by the noise.[11]

Returning to the Greeks, we find a curious reflection of the theory in one of the explanations offered for the Pythagorean prohibition of beans as an article of food. This was commonly supposed to be rooted in a mysterious affinity between beans and human beings, and one way of accounting for it was that in the beginning, when the earth was in ferment and plants and animals were being produced from her indiscriminately, men and beans arose 'from the same putrefaction'. 'Putrefaction' (in Greek *sēpedōn*) was the word used by Diodorus for the fertile cells enclosed in membranes, and it is used again here to indicate the common origin of man and the tabooed vegetable. Its use was no doubt prompted by the persistent belief that the humbler forms of animal life still arose spontaneously from rotting or putrefying animal and vegetable matter. This also is a belief which has had a remarkable history, and since it is not too irrelevant to our theme, we may look at it more closely.[12]

The belief that the first men and animals came from the earth was supported by reference to the supposed fact that the earth still retained this life-giving power to a minor degree. The claim of Egypt to have been the original home of animal life was based, according to Diodorus, on the fact that the soil of the Thebaid still at certain times generated mice. These, he says, have been seen, to the astonishment of the beholder, fully formed as far as the breast and forefeet, and capable of movement, but with the rest of the body still a shapeless clod of earth. It stands to reason that soil which is still of such surpassing richness was eminently suited to produce even men at the time when the world was still in course of formation.[13]

Philosophers before Socrates were interested above all in the question of origins. They asked how life arose in the first place, before pairing was possible, and it was in this way, as something from the distant past, that they put forward the theory of spontaneous generation from the earth. In support of it some at least of them referred to the popular belief that it could still occur; but the first serious researcher into the animal and plant life of his own day was Aristotle, and he was the first to hold as a scientific doctrine what before him had been an unquestioned belief of simple peasants. In a passage of his *History of Animals* dealing with insects (in whose life-cycle he was particularly interested) he writes:

Some of them are born from creatures of the same species, e.g. *phalangia* and *arachnia* [two sorts of spider], locusts, grasshoppers

[39]

and cicadas: others not from parents but spontaneously, some
from dew falling on leaves . . . some in putrefying mud or dung,
some in wood (either growing or dry), some in the hairs of
animals, some in their flesh, some in excretions whether
separate or still in the animal, e.g. intestinal worms.

Besides insects, other creatures spontaneously generated included
eels and certain other fish, testacea and jelly-fish. In a more
philosophic treatise on the general principles of being he says that
there are three modes of generation: natural, artificial and spontaneous. Spontaneity may even produce the same results as the
more usual processes of nature, for sometimes the same things are
produced without seed as with it. Elsewhere he says that this is
true of certain species of fish. According to Aristotle's general
philosophy all motion, change and generation has an external
cause ('nothing moves itself'), but in this special case he feels
bound to admit that matter seems to have the power of changing
itself in the same way as it is usually changed from without.
This is a negation of his general principle, and it was bad
luck that observational science was not sufficiently advanced to
enable him to dispense with it.[14]

For Aristotle, then, spontaneous generation was not prob-
lematic, but an established fact. So it was also to his pupil
Theophrastus, though he argues against it in some specific instances. He rejected, for example, a belief which may still be met in
our own day, that small frogs fall in a shower of rain. 'They do not
rain down as some think, but were previously under the earth, and
now appear because the water has run into their hiding-places.'
Nor did Theophrastus believe that any species was engendered by
spontaneous means alone, but certain plants and animals, he held,
could arise spontaneously as well as from seed. Spontaneous
generation was due to perfectly natural causes, which he expounds
in detail. Here is a typical passage from his botanical works:

Everywhere nature generates life by mixing heat with moisture in a certain way, the moisture acting as matter for the
putrefaction caused by heat. This happens e.g. with worms in
wheat. They are engendered in the roots when the sowing is

followed by excessive southerly winds, for then the root gets wet, and since the air is warm the heat produces animal life by causing the root to decay. Once born, the worm immediately devours the root, for all species live naturally on that from which they were born.

Elsewhere he explains that there are two sorts of heat, a destructive and a generative, and similarly with moisture. 'The generative agent is heat.' 'It is clear that that which propagates and brings to life is the generative moisture.' The relation between them is that heat is the agent, and moisture the matter on which it acts.[15]

When one considers such things as the visible effect of the sun's warmth on plant-growth and the return of life in spring, or the warmth of a living body and the coldness of a corpse, these views seem to be squarely based on genuine, if elementary, observation. Is it fanciful to see also an unconscious echo from the days when the fire-god was said to have produced a living being by mixing water with the dry earth? Probably not, and it is equally likely that the myths themselves were an earlier expression of the same observations.

The belief in spontaneous generation was practically universal throughout antiquity. St Augustine's version of it was that there were two kinds of seed, one implanted in animals that they might reproduce their own kinds, the other existing in the elements and becoming active under certain conditions. There is however one isolated and noteworthy assertion attributed to the Pythagoreans, that animals are born out of one another from seed and that generation from the earth is an impossibility. This for its time is really astonishing, and if it amounted to a denial of the whole belief in spontaneous generation it puts its authors ahead of most naturalists until the 19th century. Jean Fernel in the 16th still taught that the lowlier forms of life were produced by the ooze of rivers and the seashore, and bees and insects from the carcases of beasts. Two centuries later Buffon and Linnaeus were of the same mind as Augustine on the matter, although William Harvey had challenged it in the intervening period, and Francesco Redi of Florence had in the 17th century proved by experiment that the worms found in putrefying meat came from flies and not from the putrefying flesh. It took the work of Pasteur and Lister to disprove it entirely. We now know that, as Sherrington put it, 'recruitment of living from lifeless is going on in almost endless variety on land, in sea, and river, and unceasingly; but in all its instances its starting-point is already existent life'. The discovery has been of enormous benefit to mankind, for it is the assumption that germs never arise spontaneously that has made it possible to banish them, with all the pain and misery that they can cause, from surgical operations.[16]

The peculiar views of Empedocles the Sicilian deserve to be treated by themselves. This many-sided genius of the early 5th century, a Western Greek from the homeland of Pythagoreanism and the Orphic religious writers, presents an almost incredible blend of philosopher, scientist, physician, mystic, exhibitionist and poet. It is no surprise to find the philosopher-poet Lucretius extolling him as 'scarcely seeming born of mortal stock'.[17] He was unique, yet at the same time his complex mentality might be said to embody the quintessence of the transitional age, between myth and science, into which he was born. Certainly no other age or people could have produced him. His outlook is at times so rational and scientific, and at others so steeped in poetry and mystical religion, that scholars have argued endlessly over the question whether he kept his science and his religion in separate compartments of his mind, so that any attempt to reconcile them is futile, or whether they represent different phases of a magnificent philosophico-religious synthesis. These large questions are not for us to settle here, nor can we pause to admire the way in which he answered the austere logic of Parmenides by introducing into cosmology the notion of an ultimate pluralism. But a quick look at his account of the general development of the cosmos is necessary if we are to understand what he said about the origin of life.

This development is cyclic. There are four irreducible elements —earth, water, air and fire—and two irreconcilable forces working upon them. By combining and separating under the action of these forces, the elements produce the world of natural forms. These forces he calls by the mythical and picturesque names of

Love and Strife. The tendency of one is to compel the elements to unite and combine with each other. The second drives each one to seek its like and avoid the other three. When the attractive force is in full control, the sum of matter is a sphere in which the four elements are indistinguishably fused together. Since there is as yet no conception of non-material forces, the predominance is expressed in spatial terms. Strife is said to have been driven outside the sphere, while Love is within it mingling everywhere with the elements. Each however is fated to control in turn, so in due course Strife begins to penetrate the sphere and little by little to expel its contrary. The effect of this is that the elements gradually begin to separate, until with the triumph of the disruptive force they are arranged in separate layers—earth at the centre, then water and air, and fire at the circumference—and Love or attraction is driven outside. The process then repeats itself with Love gradually gaining the upper hand.[18]

Our own world is at an intermediate stage. Strife is gaining, and already great masses of the elements are separated in the form of earth and sea, with air above and the fiery stars at the circumference. But in organic nature the elements are still blended, for living creatures consist of a mixture of them in certain fixed proportions. Though the force of mutual attraction is in retreat, it is still potent.[19]

That is the general picture. Worlds are formed alternately in two opposite ways, either by the gradual coming together of elements originally separate, or (like our own) in the course of their disintegration from a state of complete fusion. Consequently, as Empedocles says, there is 'a twofold generation of mortal beings'. Take first that half of the cycle in which Strife is gaining, which is the world in which we live. This is what happened, in Empedocles's own words:

Come now, hear how fire, as it was separated, raised up the darkling shoots of miserable men and women. Not erring nor ignorant is the tale. Whole-natured forms first arose from the earth, having a portion both of water and of heat. These the fire sent up, wishing to come to its like. [I.e. under the influence of Strife the heat in the earth was drawn towards the main mass of fire at the circumference of the sphere.] Not yet did they show forth the pleasing shape of limbs, nor any voice nor the part proper to men.

As evolution proceeded under the influence of Strife, these animate lumps acquired a more articulate structure. They grew limbs, and in particular the sexes were differentiated, so that later creatures were born by sexual union, no longer from the earth.

We see how the common belief in birth out of the ground, so vividly illustrated by Diodorus's story of the mice in Egypt, is fitted by Empedocles into his highly original scheme of cosmology. The role of moisture, and that of fire as the active principle, which we have observed both in the myths and in the early rational accounts, are also retained in the universe governed by Strife. We cannot here go into all the details of its formation, but I shall mention one which exemplifies the remarkable logical consistency of the system—the way in which the general assumptions of the world-process are made to account for single details within it. Since the cosmos is being produced by the increasing ascendancy of Strife, we have seen that its evolution has been in the direction of more and more marked differentiation. When Empedocles comes to explain the particular natural fact (which he evidently knew) that a single tree may combine the two sexes, it is now easy for him to explain it on the supposition that trees emerged at an earlier stage of the world's evolution than sexually differentiated creatures.[20]

Even stranger things happened in the other half of the cosmic cycle, when the power of mutual attraction was gaining ground and forming a cosmos from the four elements in an initial state of separation. As evolution proceeded in this direction, the first appearance of life was naturally the reverse of what it had been in the early stages of the ascendancy of Strife. Instead of 'whole-natured', shapeless living masses, the different parts of animals came into being at first in separation. They were scattered about, so that in his own words 'many heads sprang up without necks, arms wandered bare for lack of shoulders and eyes strayed alone in want of foreheads'. Under the dominant urge to combine, these separate limbs and organs were at first joined together haphazard and produced monstrosities:

> Many creatures came into being with double faces and double breasts, ox-kinds with the foreparts of men, and on the other hand there sprang up men with heads of oxen, and mixed creatures partly of men and partly woman-natured.

Here Empedocles seems to be finding a place in his grand scheme for the traditions of his countrymen which told of the existence long ago of creatures like the Minotaur or the centaurs. But what is most remarkable is the strictly mechanical nature of the evolutionary process. In spite of the religious background to his thought, it leaves no room for any idea of divine purpose or intelligent creation, only the chance result of the interplay of opposed forces of attraction and repulsion on material elements. In fact his picture, bizarre as it is, contains the first hint in European thought of a doctrine of evolution by natural selection. Aristotle noted that, according to him, those creatures whose structure simulated purpose survived, but all that were not suitably constituted perished. The point is expanded by his commentator Simplicius:

> Empedocles says that during the rule of Love there came into being at random first of all parts of animals such as heads and hands and feet, and then there came together those 'ox-kinds with the foreparts of men', while on the other hand 'there sprang up', naturally, 'men with the heads of oxen', that is, compounded of ox and man. As many of these parts as were fitted together in such a way as to ensure their preservation, became animals and survived, because they fulfilled mutual needs—the teeth tearing and softening food, the stomach digesting it, and the liver converting it into blood. The human head, when it meets a human body, ensures the preservation of the whole, but being inappropriate to the ox-body it leads to its disappearance. All that did not come together according to the right formula perished.'[21]

3

Body and Soul:
the Kinship of Nature

That puff of vapour . . . man's soul.
(BROWNING)

We may now widen our scope a little, considering some Greek ideas about the nature of life rather than only its origins. This will probably be necessary even for our primary object, an understanding of how the Greeks supposed it to have started. There seems to be a formal ambiguity in the modern scientific position. The great biologist Sir Charles Sherrington, from whom I have quoted already, wrote that 'natural science has studied life to the extent of explaining away life as any radically separate category of phenomena. The categories of living and lifeless as regards science disappear; there is no radical scientific difference between living and dead.' Again, referring to the difficulty experienced by Aristotle and later biologists in finding the boundary between the animate and the inanimate, he said: 'Today's scheme makes plain why that difficulty was, and dissolves it. There is no boundary.' Elsewhere however he mentions criteria by which living are distinguished from other energy-systems—they are much the same criteria as Aristotle used: nutrition, growth, reproduction and so on—and agrees that the word remains useful: 'a convenient, though not exact, term'. It is of course still in use, among scientists as well as laymen. 'The origin of life' is a phrase that has meaning for scientists. Indeed the American Association for the Advancement of Science recently held a dis-

[46]

cussion about it, and an international congress is to meet in Moscow this year for the express purpose of studying it.[1]

The ancient Greeks, or some of them, were in a similarly ambiguous position, though for very different reasons. There was a sense in which, to some of their early philosophers, the boundary between animate and inanimate was non-existent. It is of course well known that there is an early stage of human thought, still represented by some peoples today, which naively looks on everything as alive. In this state of mind, which the anthropologist Tylor christened animism, everything is endowed with a soul as well as a body, and rivers, stones or trees may act with good or evil intent, may be offended, persuaded or propitiated. The popular religion of Greece had certainly not outgrown this stage. For the earliest philosophers it was dead, but perhaps its ghost still haunted their speculations unperceived.

I said earlier that Thales and his companions in Ionia supposed the world to have arisen from a homogeneous mass of matter which was in everlasting motion. The production of variety out of the original uniformity was achieved through this primal movement. But why was it in motion? What caused it to move? To this problem, Aristotle complained, they had no answer.[2] It would be better to say that the problem did not as yet exist. Crudely put, the answer which they assumed—though they did not think of it as the answer to any question—was that the primal matter was alive. It was not what we should call inanimate matter: it was the *sole* source of the universe, matter and cause in one, for it initiated its own changes. To express this the Milesians have been given the rather forbidding title of hylozoists, which simply means 'life-in-matter' philosophers. Today a scientist can deny the distinction between living and non-living, meaning that it has already been asserted but modern discoveries have revealed its inadequacy; but here at the dawn of rational thought we meet people for whom the distinction has not yet made itself felt. We saw how for Aristotle the most probable explanation of Thales's choice of water as sole principle lay in the indispensable part which it plays in conception, birth and nutrition; and also how this supposition was borne out by older Egyptian ideas with which Thales would have been familiar. As for Anaximander's infinite and indefinite world-substance, this is how Aristotle writes of it:

Everything either *is* an origin or *has* an origin: the Unlimited has no origin, for that would be a limit of it. Moreover being an origin [or source or principle: Greek *arche*], it is ungenerated and imperishable. .... Therefore as I say, there is no origin for it, but it appears to be the origin of other things, and to encompass all things and direct all things, as those philosophers say who do not posit besides the Unlimited other causes such as Mind or Love; and this they say is the divine, for it is immortal and imperishable, as Anaximander and most of the writers on nature call it.'[3]

The same mysterious x, which is what we might call the material substratum of the world, is also the force which guides or directs it. It is not only everlasting, but everlastingly alive, immortal and divine.

There was a third member of this Milesian school, Anaximenes the pupil of Anaximander. He attacked the problem on the same assumptions—i.e. the unity and the self-moving nature of the ultimate stuff of the universe—and concluded that the origin of all things was from air. He took an important step forward, for he consciously sought a known natural process which might account for all physical change, and found it in the effects of condensation and rarefaction. He saw, as he thought, the invisible air become visible as mist and cloud under the condensing influence of a drop in temperature. He saw the clouds fall as rain and the water turn to ice. Conversely he saw that water when heated, and so expanded, first turned to vapour and then became invisible. By an extension of these processes he supposed it to ignite as fire at one extreme, and at the other to solidify into earth and stones. In the end the world and all that it contains were the product of this one substance, which he called air and believed to exist in its most equably balanced state in the form of the invisible atmosphere.[4]

He too assumed an uncaused, everlasting motion, and there were good reasons in earlier Greek thought why he should have attributed this to the air. First, to a Greek self-motion of necessity suggested life: it is scarcely too much to say that in popular as well as philosophic thought this power was the one fundamental criterion for distinguishing living from non-living. Secondly, in the popular thought of Anaximenes's time and earlier, life and the breath of life were intimately connected if not identified. The breath-soul is a world-wide conception. The ordinary Greek word for soul, *psyche*, means also breath, as does the Latin *anima*. According to the religious poetry of the Orphics, known to Aristotle, 'the soul enters into us from the whole as we breathe, borne by the winds'. Related to this was the belief that female animals could be impregnated by inhaling the winds.[5]

Our knowledge of these early philosophers is sadly circumscribed by the fact that their own writings have perished. The authorities that we possess wrote from a wide variety of motives and their accuracy is difficult to assess. There is no need for scepticism, however, when we read that Anaximenes thought of the air as god, and also drew an analogy between the air which sustains the universe and the human soul. The idea that the whole world is a living and breathing creature was firmly upheld by the Pythagoreans, and finds its most striking expression in Plato's *Timaeus*. In one of those summaries of earlier views which depend ultimately on the history of Aristotle's pupil Theophrastus, we read:

> Anaximenes of Miletus, son of Eurystratus, declared that the origin of existing things is air. Out of it all things come to be and into it they are resolved again. He says that just as our soul, which is air, holds us together, so breath and air surround the whole cosmos. Air and breath are used synonymously.[6]

Thus everything is made of one substance, and that substance, at least in its most properly balanced, invisible form, is the substance of life. Since it is everlastingly alive, it is divine, for immortality and divinity were also two inseparable concepts for a Greek. The life-principle in finite living creatures is the same. Perhaps that is what Thales meant in one of the few sayings which can be plausibly assigned to him: 'Everything is full of gods.'[7]

A philosopher of the 5th century, Diogenes of Apollonia, took up and developed the views of Anaximenes. He wrote:

D   [49]

Mankind and the other animals live on air, by breathing; and it is to them both soul and mind.

The soul of all animals is the same, namely air which is warmer than the air outside, in which we live, though much colder than that near the sun.

In my opinion that which has intelligence is what men call air, and by it everything is directed, and it has power over all things; for it is just this substance which I hold to be God.

Theophrastus puts his doctrine in the form that 'the air within us is a small portion of the god'. This doctrine is parodied by Aristophanes, when in one of his comedies he brings Socrates on to the stage suspended in the air in a basket. Asked the reason for this strange proceeding, Socrates replies that to discover the truth about celestial matters, he must allow his mind to mingle with the *kindred* air. [8]

The belief sounds materialistic, but is so only in the sense that its holders knew of no distinction between the material and the spiritual, not in the sense that, like a modern materialist, they knew and rejected the idea of the non-material. Since it taught that man's soul was consubstantial with the divinity that governed the universe, it obviously offered scope for development in the direction of mystical religion. But although at this stage religion and natural philosophy cannot be wholly separated, we shall try to follow rather its implications for the science of the day.

Blest as they were with a climate bathed in brilliant light, the Greeks distinguished two layers in the atmosphere. The less pure, which filled the space up to cloud level and included mist, fog, and the air we breathe, was called *aer*. The purer substance in the upper reaches was *aither*. Sometimes this word seems to mean air, and sometimes fire. Until Aristotle, or someone shortly before him, gave it philosophic recognition as a fifth element alongside the other four, its status varied. Its root meaning is 'blazing', and it was formally identified with fire by Anaxagoras, the scientific friend of Pericles who was prosecuted for saying that the sun was not a god but an incandescent lump of stone larger than the Peloponnese. [9]

This *aither* had definite associations both with divinity and with life. It was the home of Zeus. It was even said that Zeus was only the name that men gave to the *aither*—not unnaturally, since he was the god of the sky. It was also the stuff of which the stars were made. All this was linked with human life in a belief that at death the soul flew off to join the *aither*. The official epitaph on the Athenians who fell in the battle of Potidaea said: '*Aither* received their souls; their bodies, earth.' 'Body to earth, breath to the *aither*,' says a character in Euripides, and another: 'He is quenched like a fallen star, releasing his breath to the *aither*.' Again: 'The mind of the dead lives not perhaps, yet has it an immortal power of thought, when it has plunged into the immortal *aither*.' The simile of the star is significant, for a line of Aristophanes reveals it as a popular superstition that the stars are the souls of dead men.[10]

We can now link together various elements in a complex of thought. From Anaximander onwards, the natural philosophers held that in the separation of the elements at the formation of the world, fire took the outermost place. There, at the confines of space, is its natural home, and the upward movement of flame here on earth only confirms that its natural tendency is to seek the same regions. It should be added that for the philosophers fire in its unmixed form was not visible flame, but rather the purest essence of 'the hot and the dry'. Heraclitus went so far as to say that the whole cosmos is 'an ever-living fire', and he clearly did not mean that it burns like the bush which Moses saw. He said that the human soul is most intensely alive, and most intelligent, when it is warmest and dryest, evidently because in this state it comes closest to the pure cosmic fire which was divinity. Putting it in his own terms, Aristotle concluded that for Heraclitus the soul was an exhalation. His commentator John Philoponus expanded this by saying that the soul was made of fire, but that this was what Heraclitus meant by fire—not flame, but a dry exhalation.[11]

Fire or *aither* is the purest form of substance, and the purest form of substance is the seat of everlasting life. On earth we are tied to bodies which are made of grosser matter and subject to dissolution. But the soul is distinct from the body. In this lowly situation, it is best described as airy rather than aetherial, but at death it may rise purified into the *aither* itself, merged in the divinity of the universe. Plato uses the distinction between *aer* and *aither* to point a moral. Then as now, men believed in ghosts, and were ready to swear that they had seen them, particularly in the neighbourhood of tombs. Yes, says Plato, these are the souls of those who in life clogged their substance with the gross pleasures of the body. As a result they cannot free themselves from it all at once, they are saturated with its humours and still corporeal in nature, and that is why they can still be seen. We may assume that their substance is the darkly visible *aer*, not yet the pure *aither*.[12]

I have mentioned Anaxagoras, the freethinker who said that not only the sun, but all the stars, were only white-hot stones. These brilliant circling luminaries, whose divinity had been implicitly believed from time immemorial, were no more than inanimate lumps. Their life had been confidently inferred from their unceasing motion. What moves is animate. Not so, said Anaxagoras. The universe is surrounded by a whirling mass of *aither*, which is fiery in its nature, and by the vigour of its motion it has caught up rocks from the earth and set them on fire. That is how the stars were made.[13] It should be interesting to see how so bold and original a mind, with so little respect for traditional beliefs, treats the question of life. The evidence is scanty, but there is some, and since the air has a part to play in it, it may as well be considered here. But a little more is necessary first to characterize the man and the world-system within which he depicted life as arising.

By now Greek thought had advanced far enough to be concerned about the problem of a first cause, which as we saw did not trouble the minds of the earliest cosmologists. The idea of a material which moved itself was no longer satisfactory. Now if reason appears to demand a first cause, then however rational and unmoved by religious prejudices a cosmologist may be, he is inevitably committed to a non-material and deistic conception. The universe is made up of a certain sum of matter, and the notion is beginning to assert itself that this matter, left to itself, is inert. But it moves and changes. On these premises, what moves it must be something other than matter, and its action cannot be purely physical and mechanical, as one moving piece of matter can push or pull another. Anaxagoras faced these consequences, and said that the first cause was Mind. Whether he had actually achieved the notion of completely incorporeal existence is sometimes doubted, but at least he emphasized the fact that it stood apart from the mixture of which the universe was made, being itself 'mixed with no thing'. On the other hand he limited its operation to the minimum, so much so that Plato and Aristotle with their teleological outlook complained bitterly that although he called the first cause Mind, he did not, as one would then expect, depict the world as being ordered throughout on rational lines, as the fulfilment of a divine purpose. He simply used Mind as a device to start things off, and then discarded it. It had nothing to do with the detailed ordering of the universe, which Anaxagoras accounted for by the purely physical and unpurposed action of *aither*, air, water and so forth. In his own words, 'When Mind had started the movement, it began to withdraw from the moving whole.'[14]

Anaxagoras put forward an original and highly complicated theory of matter, the exact purport of which, owing no doubt to gaps in our evidence, is something on which scholars have failed to agree. But a few indubitable points may be mentioned as background to his reported views on living things. His view is the antithesis of that of Empedocles, according to whom the great masses of earth, water, air and fire are simple and elemental, and organic bodies are compounds of these. Anaxagoras retained the idea, common to the poets and to his philosophic predecessors, that the original state of things was a chaos in which everything was mixed up with everything else. Like others before him also, he posited a rotatory motion in this primal mass which brought about separation, and it is in terms of this separating-out of an original mixture that the genesis of the world is to be conceived. The rotation was started by the external moving cause, Mind, which, he said, was no part of the mixture; but once started, the process goes on under its own momentum much as it did for Anaximander.[15]

But now comes the second innovation. Like Empedocles,

Anaxagoras was seeking to overcome the difficulty raised by another thinker, Parmenides, who seemed to have shown by strict logic that nothing could in an absolute sense ever come into being or perish. The solution of Empedocles was to say that the only true substances were the four elements. They were everlasting, and organic bodies were formed by their mixture in different proportions. What men call birth and death are only the mingling and separation of non-perishable substances. Anaxagoras felt compelled to lay down a stricter condition. All the different natural substances like flesh, bone, tissue, hair, wood, metals, and so forth must be truly substantial. Any explanation, therefore, of natural birth, growth and death must start from the axiom that, whatever appearances may say to the contrary, none of these really comes into existence at any time, or really perishes. On these assumptions, and in a pre-chemical age, it is clearly going to be a problem to explain the growth of a human being from the size of an embryo to a six-foot tall adult, and it is this kind of problem which seems to have especially fascinated Anaxagoras. Aristotle describes the position as follows:

> The schools of Anaxagoras and Empedocles are opposed to each other: Empedocles says that fire, water, air and earth are four elements, and it is they that are simple rather than flesh, bone, and similar homoeomerous substances; but the followers of Anaxagoras assert that these substances are simple and elemental, whereas earth, fire, water and air are compounds, being made up of particles of the others.[16]

The disentangling of the original chaos is a gradual process, and according to Anaxagoras the formation of the four so-called elements is a very early stage. These great masses are in fact confused agglomerations of miscellaneous substances which still cohere in the form of particles (or 'seeds' as he called them) so tiny that the distinctive nature of each separate substance is imperceptible. In the original chaos these infinitesimal particles had been so thoroughly mixed that no differences could be perceived at all. In earth, water, air and fire, they are so far sorted out as to exhibit separately the primary qualities of dry and wet, cold and hot, but any more precise distinctions are still in the future. (Similarly in Anaximander's system, we may remember, it is these distinctions which first make their appearance in the Unlimited.) These further distinctions become manifest as the evolution of the world proceeds, and by a process of the attraction of like to like, the particles of, say, bone or wood come together in quantities sufficient for them to be recognizable for what they are and distinguished from gold or silver or grass. The application of this to the particular problem of nutrition and growth is that the things on which we feed, like wheat, milk, or olives, must be supposed to contain flesh, bone, blood and everything else which goes to make up an animal body, in quantities so minute as to be below the level of perception. The wheat which we eat does not *turn into* flesh—for in the process an elemental substance, wheat, would have perished —but the body absorbs the particles of flesh which were concealed in it, and rids itself of the rest. It is these innumerable substances of the natural world that are the real elements. The earth and the air are nothing in themselves. They are only heterogeneous masses in which the elements cohere, but no single element in sufficient quantity in one place for its individual nature to appear.[17]

What then, on the basis of this general system, did he think about the origins of life? We may say in the first place, although his works are lost, that he was obviously interested in biological and physiological questions. (Incidentally Plato tells us in the *Apology* that at the time of Socrates's trial, Anaxagoras's book could be bought at Athens for a drachma. It was still available to Simplicius in the 6th century A.D.) He discussed, for instance, the point at which distinction of sex is decided in the individual, whether at the moment of conception or later, and interested himself in the mechanism of respiration in fish. About the origin of life, we are told first of all that in general terms he adhered to what might be called the 'Pandora' theory. In the myth, you remember, the fire-god took earth and water to make a living human being. Anaxagoras subscribed to the view that 'animals were born from wet, hot, and earthy substance, and later on from each other'. For any further detail of how it happened, we have little more than a single brief sentence on which we can rely, but that sentence is important. Theophrastus writes of Anaxagoras as saying that 'the air contains the seeds of all things and that these are brought down together with the water and generate plants'.[18]

What an original mind Anaxagoras had—and yet how can we help being reminded of much older ideas? To us the word 'fertilize' has two senses. We speak of irrigating a desert to make it fertile, meaning thereby that the water will create favourable conditions for the germination of seeds. The seeds must still be put there in the first place. It is in another sense that a female is fertilized by a male. For us the rain only fertilizes in the first sense, by supplying the moisture necessary for the germination and growth of seeds already present and in a state to germinate. But we have seen that in the myths it was by raining on her that the sky actually wedded and impregnated the earth. The rain was the seed. So it is in his own way for Anaxagoras. His genius had conceived of *aer*—air or cloud or mist—not as being a separate element, but as containing in suspension all the substances which went to make up plants and animals, as well as others. What more natural than that, when cloud condenses into water and falls as rain, this rain should wash down with it the tiny compound nuclei, or seeds, which will develop into the earliest forms of life on earth?

In this sentence Theophrastus speaks only of plant life, but we may be confident that Anaxagoras thought of the first animals as having been born in the same way. This certainly does not conflict with his acceptance of the prevailing opinion that they were born spontaneously from 'the wet, the hot and the earthy', and it is actually attributed to him by a source on whom one would not perhaps like to rely without support, the 2nd-century Christian bishop Irenaeus. His words are: 'Anaxagoras, who was called atheist, insisted that animals were created by the fall of seeds from the sky to the earth.' Plutarch moreover classed him with Plato and Democritus as one of those who saw a very close relationship between plant and animal life, describing plants as 'earthbound animals'. We may even give credit, so far as it goes, to a misleadingly brief note in one of those late summaries of philosophical doctrines that go back in the last resort to Theophrastus's history. This is to the effect that like Anaximenes, Diogenes of Apollonia, and Archelaus, he (or his followers) said that the soul or life principle (*psyche*) was air-like. The basis of Anaxagoras's theory was far more subtle than that of Anaximenes, and his statement that the germs of life came to earth from the air was supported by a much more precise explanation; but that life did come from the air was true for both of them. In fact Anaxagoras borrowed much in his cosmology from his Ionian predecessor, including the association of hot with rare and cold with dense. He even said— and here we have his actual words—that the prevailing character of the original mixture, in which 'nothing was apparent owing to smallness', was that of infinite *aer* and *aither*. In a sense, then, he borrowed from Anaximenes the notion that all things come from air, but he had his own theory of the composition of that air.[19]

It is time to make explicit an idea which has already been implied by much that I have said in this chapter, the idea of the kinship of all life. Like other ideas that we have been considering, it has its pre-rational form and its scientific form. Prevalent among those to whom magic is still a potent force, it reappears among the highest intellects of Greece. In our own century it has again received scientific recognition, after a period of eclipse which has been partly due to certain forms of Christian teaching and the adoption of Aristotelianism in the scholastic and ossified form of which Aristotle himself would certainly not have approved. In Sherrington's book we read: 'New knowledge has put us in a new perspective. Other life is in a sense drawn greatly closer to us. It is not now another order of being, but our own kith and kin. Their nature and ours are one.'[20] It is indeed new knowledge that has done this for us, and that is something we must never forget. At the same time there is a certain interest in seeing how the mind of man drew him, before this knowledge was available, to conclusions in some ways similar. This kind of historical reflection may even, as I suggested at the beginning, put us on our guard against assuming that new knowledge must inevitably lead to certain conclusions, when in fact we are in some cases unconsciously organizing that knowledge in accordance with certain preconceptions inherited from a distant past.

The kinship of all nature was a familiar idea to the Greeks. Anaxagoras thought of plants as earthbound animals. Plato wrote that they are 'a substance of a kindred nature to man's', and that they 'live and are no different from other living creatures, except that they are rooted and static'. But it was the Pythagoreans who exalted the kinship of nature into a primary principle of their philosophy, and the phrase was almost certainly used by Pythagoras himself.[21] It has its roots in magic, and the connexion is plainly seen in Pythagoreanism, a system which blended in an extraordinary way the primitive and the philosophic. A common form of belief in magic rests on the assumption of sympathy or affinity, a close and squasi-physical relationship between things which to the civilized mind have no such connexion at all. It makes possible all sorts of action at a distance, thus introducing the necessity of ordering one's own life on principles quite other than those that prevail among ourselves. The same sort of affinity is seen in a totemic organization of society, in which a tribe is conscious of a kinship, even an identity, between itself and a certain species of animal, and a code of conduct and taboo is built on this belief. Sympathy of this kind between the movements of the stars and the nature of man is of course the basis of astrology.

This wide conception of kinship or sympathy, in a more or less rationalized form, is central to the philosophy of Pythagoras and his followers. We have already noted their belief in a mysterious common origin for mankind and beans, in connexion with which there were many curious superstitions. It was said for instance that a bean if buried in the earth, or in dung, would assume human shape. The belief in kinship made possible Pythagoras's characteristic doctrine of the transmigration of souls between man and animals, and it is prominent a little later in Empedocles, who explicitly extended it to plants. Consistency of thought is difficult to achieve in such matters, and just how much should be included in the strict bond of unity was something on which not all were agreed. The question was not merely academic. Both for the Pythagoreans and for Empedocles the kinship between man and animals involved abstention from eating meat, for a man who consumes beef may unwittingly be eating his father, whose soul may have entered and animated the bull. And in his treatise on abstinence from flesh, which makes use of much ancient Pythagorean material, the Neoplatonic philosopher Porphyry feels the necessity of opposing the extreme view that even vegetables are to be avoided, since all life is akin. Some Pythagoreans evidently found a way out by drawing a distinction between life and soul. The basis of all life is warmth. Plants are alive, but do not possess soul (*psyche*), which is a particular combination of hotter and colder *aither* and is immortal, because the *aither* is immortal.[22]

It might be thought that at least for the early monist philosophers, everything must be alive, since the whole world is made of one substance and that, like Anaximenes's air, is living and self-moving. We know too little of their systems to say whether this kind of logical consistency is to be expected from them. Possibly they did think of it as simply a question of degree. One seems to see glimpses of a common basis of belief, but conjecture must play a considerable part in its reconstruction. Nor must we overlook the individuality of each philosopher, which means that any resemblance can only be very general. With these reservations, we may say that, in general, the essential for life was a measure of heat. If the life-principle was air for Anaximenes, it was at its dimmest when that substance was chilled, condensed and hardened as in a stone. For Anaximander it was only under the influence of heat that the moist ooze engendered living things. For Heraclitus the divine and rational principle was fire, and individual souls were most alive when hot, and nearest to death when cold and wet. In the atomic materialism of Democritus, the atoms of soul most closely resembled those of fire. We have already noticed the widespread belief in the kinship of the soul with *aither*. In its colder, harder and more solid forms, matter lost its power of self-motion—that is, its life—and so, even for these pre-Platonic thinkers who had as yet drawn no distinction between material and non-material, the life-principle resided in a particular form of matter characterized by mobility. In atomism, this generalization took the form of saying that the soul was composed of the smallest, smoothest and roundest atoms. It was a sort of quicksilver. The atoms of the body were large, rough, irregular or hooked. They clung together in solid, sluggish masses, and the soul-atoms animated and moved them. Democritus liked to draw a sharp distinction between body and soul, calling the body only the soul's tenement and in his ethical teaching exalting the attributes of soul over those of body—for soul is the seat of the moral virtues and of thought. At the same time, so long as it is thought of as something material, it is difficult to make the distinction absolute, and there is one curious statement attributed to Democritus which suggests that he failed to do so. He held, says our authority, that all things share in soul of a kind, even dead bodies, because they still retain a portion of heat and of the sensitive faculty when the greater part has been dispersed in the air. There were also religious dogmas, like those of the Pythagoreans and Orphics, which sharply distinguished soul from body and despised the latter; but since for them too, in all probability, the soul was of a fiery or aetherial substance, we must say that a truly spiritual conception of it was not possible until Plato and Aristotle familiarized philosophy with the notion of incorporeal being.[23]

This brief summary of a few early Greek attempts to elucidate the mystery of life has only touched the fringes of a very large subject. I hope at least that I have not over-simplified to the extent of being misleading. I will sum up by picking out a few leading ideas which are perhaps of more than passing interest.

1. We notice first that, in trying to think back to the origins of life, these men leaned heavily on analogy with what goes on today. Since to them spontaneous generation from the earth or decaying matter was a fact of every-day experience, it naturally seemed to offer the best clue to what happened in the beginning. We saw from Diodorus that the claim of Egypt to have been the original home of life was substantiated in this way. He also compared the original life-producing pustules on the surface of the still plastic earth to the bubbles now produced in swamps by eruptions of marsh-gas. The point is put generally by a later writer who drew largely on the same early sources as Diodorus, though his account follows the Platonic tradition of a divine creator. 'It is no marvel,'

writes this man, 'that earth mixed with water should in the beginning have formed animals and plants, in accordance with the mind of the Creator. It is natural that air or breath (*pneuma*) should be contained in water, and vital heat in the air; and it is proved by the creatures which come to birth in the hollows of the earth or those which are born of putrefaction.'[24] The same analogy from present to past is seen in the argument that, just as now an infant is nourished by milk from its mother, so in the beginning, before animals had parents of their own kind, their common mother the earth must have provided an analogous liquid to sustain them. Again, the parts played by the sun's heat and by moisture in sustaining and developing life today led to the conviction that heat as active principle, and moisture as a vehicle, must have been the two essentials in the first creation of life.

In using this analogy from present to past, the Greek thinkers were adopting the only possible course. Even today, the scientist who interests himself in the origins of life must take a holiday from the laboratory. A zoologist has recently written: 'We have to rely on the assumption that the sort of processes we can study now were also the processes at work in the first living things.' 'It is a fascinating intellectual exercise, for the hypotheses cannot be proved false by the usual test of experiment, but only by superior reasoning or by logical demonstration that some new factor has been overlooked.'[25]

2. A second analogy constantly employed by the Greeks was that from microcosm to macrocosm. In different ways, and to different degrees, they thought of the world itself as alive, and this universal life-principle was the same as that operative in terrestrial creatures, though in them it might be blunted and weakened by contamination with grosser forms of matter. In particular the analogy was drawn between the earth as mother and the motherhood of a woman. This analogy extends far back to the days when Earth was personified as a great life-giving goddess, but it persisted into the period of rational thought and could be illustrated endlessly. The primeval milk-like ooze was one example. Another is the theory that as it grew older, the earth lost its capacity to bear

new life, just as a woman does. The bubble-like excrescences on the surface of the youthful earth were called wombs, and so forth.

3. The last point to which I should like to draw your attention is the evolutionary character of these theories. With the knowledge at their disposal, we cannot expect thinkers of the 6th and 5th centuries B.C. to produce a broadly-based scientific theory of evolution, but at least we find a state of mind which welcomes the idea as a natural explanation of the facts, and is not inhibited from it either by religious considerations or by any preconception of an immutable order of species. The beginnings of life take their place as a natural event in the series which started when the whole world began to evolve from a chaotic mass of matter. It was produced in due course by the same internal causes that dried out the earth, covered it with the sea, and set the heavenly bodies wheeling in the sky around it. Anaximander pictures the earliest forms of life as crawling painfully, shell-encrusted, out of the sea. Empedocles imagines creatures of no contemporary species fighting for their lives against adverse conditions and disappearing in the struggle. It was, one must admit, Aristotle who burdened science for centuries with the dogma of the fixity of species. It is strange to have to say this of the man who emphasized so strongly the difficulty of drawing a line between living and non-living. He wrote that nature exhibits a continuous progression between the two, and that the border is imperceptible. Yet he saw no need to convert this static continuity, in which one form of existence differs only minutely from the next, into a dynamic progression or evolution in time. This conviction of the immutability of species, like that of the eternity of the cosmos, was bound up for him with wider philosophical questions, doctrines of form and substance in which he developed and crystallized the Platonic elements in his intellectual heritage. But those are matters for another occasion.[26]

4

Cycles of Existence: the Golden Age

Damnosa quid non imminuit dies?

HORACE

I have just remarked, with some emphasis, on the evolutionary character of early Greek theories about the origins of the world and of life. No Greek, whether rationalist philosopher or religious poet, thought of the world as created in seven days by the fiat of an omnipotent god. This did not however exclude another idea, to which the Greek mind was especially attracted: the idea that as in space, so in time, the cosmic movement was circular. Everything returns to what it was before, and what has been will be again. As their ancient poets had taught them, not only does 'everything come to be out of one thing', but 'it is resolved into one again', and the process recommences. This was almost certainly the belief of Anaximander, and the remarkable philosophico-religious scheme of Empedocles shows how it could be combined with an evolutionary conception in the appropriate portions of the cycle. The idea of time as cyclic was an extension from the observable succession of the years, in which the seasons are endlessly repeated. Spring gives way to summer and summer in its turn to autumn and winter, but we know that spring will come again, and where we have seen the vegetation wither and die, the earth will once more be covered with the fresh green of new life exactly as it was in the year that has past. The plants which spring up will not of course be the *same* plants, and there will be many minor differences. A good year may be followed by a bad one, wheat may grow where barley grew before. Some, like Aristotle, contented themselves with projecting into history this (as they called it) specific recurrence, or recurrence in kind. It was the poignant contrast between seasonal recurrence and the finality of individual death which caught the fancy of Horace and found expression in a haunting ode—an ode, moreover, which has been fortunate in its translator.

> The snows are fled away, leaves on the shaws
> And grasses in the mead renew their birth.
> The river to the river-bed withdraws,
> And altered is the fashion of the earth.
>
> Thaw follows frost; hard on the heel of spring
> Treads summer sure to die, for hard on hers
> Comes autumn with his apples scattering;
> Then back to wintertide, when nothing stirs.
>
> But oh, whate'er the sky-led seasons mar,
> Moon upon moon rebuilds it with her beams;
> Come we where Tullus and where Ancus are
> And good Aeneas, we are dust and dreams.

Others, among whom the Pythagoreans are especially mentioned, went so far as to believe that history repeated itself in every detail. 'If we are to believe them,' said Eudemus, Aristotle's pupil, to his class, 'you will sit in front of me again and I shall be talking to you and holding this stick, just as we are now.'[1]

The idea took different forms. For the Pythagoreans it was of course bound up with the cycle of incarnations, and also with the notion of a Great Year. This too was differently explained and variously estimated. It arose from early attempts to construct a workable calendar by discovering a period of years which would coincide with an exact number of months; that is, by co-ordinating the apparent motions of the sun and moon only. But Plato and others described it as the much longer period necessary for sun, moon, and planets as well to reach again the same positions in relation to each other as they occupied at a given moment. It was very variously estimated. As Plato describes the Great Year, there is no suggestion that it led to any vast catastrophe, whether a destruction of the whole universe or a partial, terrestrial disaster like a flood. Aristotle on the other hand does connect the legendary flood with the idea that 'just as there is a winter every year, so after a certain long period of time there is a great winter with an excess of rain'.[2] There probably existed in some circles a belief in an endless repetition of history without such dramatic reversals, though how it came about we cannot say, for there is little or no information. In any case, for our present theme of origins, two other theories are more relevant, one of which need only be mentioned. We have met it already. This is the belief that our universe had a beginning in time, emerging gradually out of infinite chaos by a natural process which in due course gave rise to the various forms of life within it. That it would one day come to an end again, and in due course another universe be born, appears clearly in Empedocles, and was probably argued, from different assumptions, by others. But the question of the end of all things (perhaps naturally) does not seem to have interested these philosophers so much as did their beginning, and for our present purpose we also may neglect it.

What concerns us more closely, as we approach the story of human civilization, is another variant of the cyclic conception. Not all Greek thinkers supposed the universe to have had a beginning in time. Diodorus in the 1st century B.C. divides his predecessors thus:

> Two views about the origin of mankind have been current among the most notable scientists and historians. One school, premising that the cosmos is ungenerated and indestructible, declares that the human race has always existed, and there was no time when it began to reproduce itself. The other holds that the cosmos has been generated and may be destroyed, and that men similarly first came into existence at a definite time.[3]

The most noteworthy believer in the eternity of the universe was of course Aristotle, and he makes frequent mention of the cyclic theory of human affairs of which I want to speak. But it occurs too in his master Plato, and also in later writers like Polybius and Lucretius. Such stories, exemplified by the myth of Deucalion and Pyrrha, must have been current long before the days of philosophy, and they were used by Plato and others somewhat as tales of desert islands in the recent past—or as a modern writer might depict the recovery of life after the use of thermonuclear weapons in a future world war—to illustrate the capabilities of human ingenuity when thrown entirely on its own resources. In particular they served as a starting-point for those who wished to air their views on the origins of civilization and government. Plato gives the impression that he is recounting them as an allegory of the material and psychological springs of social life rather than a narrative of actual historical events, and yet Aristotle believed in all seriousness that the arts and sciences had been brought to perfection many times in history and then almost entirely lost and forgotten in the aftermath of some overwhelming catastrophe.

To start with one of the clearest examples, I will abandon chronological order and quote from Polybius, the Greek historian who lived in Republican Rome of the 2nd century B.C.

What then are the beginnings, and what is the source, from which constitutions come into existence? We may answer that question by saying that when a deluge, or a plague, or a failure of crops or some other similar cause has resulted in the destruction of much of the human race, as the records tell us has already happened and as reason suggests to us may often happen again, all the traditions and arts will simultaneously perish; but when in the course of time a new population has grown up again from the survivors left by the disaster, as a crop grows up from seed in the ground, a revival of social life will begin.

From this beginning Polybius proceeds to expound his theory that monarchy is the earliest form of government. It is interesting that he feels an urge to make the comparison with the growth of a crop in the ground, for as we have seen, that men did grow 'like a crop in the ground' was the *alternative* theory of human origins. Aristotle speaks of 'the first men, whether they were earth-born or the

[66]

survivors from some fatal calamity'. The latter we know to have been his own view.[4]

The belief may be further illustrated from the beginning of Plato's *Timaeus*. Here he tells the story of Solon's visit to Egypt, and how a priest of that country explained to him that the Greeks were a very young people, since in common with the majority of mankind, their predecessors had been practically wiped out by one of the periodic catastrophes which beset the earth. The peculiar situation of Egypt on the Nile protects her from these, and consequently the Egyptian temples have accumulated records of human civilization going back far beyond those possessed by any other nation. There have been, explains the priest, many destructions of mankind, some by torrid heat due to a change in the course of the heavenly bodies round the earth. The myth of Phaethon, who was allowed to drive the sun's chariot and nearly burned up the earth by his unskilful handling of the horses, has according to the priest preserved what we should nowadays call the Greek folk-memory of this natural event. Others were caused by floods, of which there have been many, though Greek memory is so short that it only knows of one. This flood was the most recent of these catastrophes, and since in a flood it is the city-dwellers and all who live in plains or by rivers who are wiped out, the survivors were only a handful of ignorant and unlettered herdsmen on the mountains. For many generations (Plato adds in the *Critias*) their energies were absorbed in procuring the necessities of life, and they had no time or inclination for the arts of civilization, which were only gradually and painfully recovered.[5]

How far Plato believed this kind of thing it is difficult to say. Certainly when he repeats it in the *Laws*, it seems to be only as a peg on which to hang some speculations about the origins and development of society from primitive times. Book 3 opens with the question: 'What is the origin of political government?' The speaker says that the best approach is the historical and temporal, and suggests that they start from the old traditions which tell of 'many destructions of mankind by flood, disease and other causes, from which only a remnant survive'. Let us imagine (νοήσωμεν) one of these, he goes on, namely the Flood. He then pictures the survivors as 'a few hill shepherds, tiny sparks of humanity surviving on mountain peaks', and goes on to consider their mode of life with a few goats or oxen as their fellow-survivors, lacking all tools and the skill to use them. It is from such a state of things that cities, governments, laws, arts and industry as we know them must be supposed to have started, and the problem is to trace the gradual evolution that this implies.[6] One would conclude that what Plato has in mind is simply the evolution of civilization from its first beginnings. The legend that it had all existed many times before, but been wiped out, is only a part of the mythology of his people of which he makes use, as he was always glad to do, to add liveliness and interest to his theories. Whether this conclusion is right is the kind of question that is constantly being raised by the imaginative form in which Plato chose to cast his thoughts, and few of us, I imagine, would choose to be rid of our doubts at the cost of having only philosophical treatises from his pen instead of the richly poetic texture of the dialogues.

Philosophical treatises of the most prosaic kind are all that we have left from Aristotle. Yet as we have seen, he believed in the Flood, and it is a favourite thesis of his that philosophy and the arts have many times flourished and again disappeared. He is quoted as saying in a lost work that proverbs are the residue of vanished philosophy. Their brevity and wit have allowed them to survive the great destructions of mankind in which the rest of human wisdom perished. In the *Metaphysics* he writes similarly that in all likelihood every art and all philosophies have been many times discovered and lost again, only a few traces surviving into the present age. This assertion he often repeats, as for instance in the *Meteorologica*: 'We must say that the same opinions have arisen among men in cycles, not once, twice, nor a few times, but infinitely often.'[7]

This tradition of the recurrent destruction of civilization by a series of natural catastrophes, and its painful rebirth among the survivors and their descendants, seemed too curious and interesting to be passed over. Features of it, including the strange idea of a recurrence of history in every detail, had their life prolonged in the Stoic theory of the periodic destruction of the cosmos in a conflagration. But for the purpose of discovering what the Greeks thought about our social origins and development it does not matter whether they came about in this way or once and for all. The tradition of development is similar whether it is introduced, as in Plato, by a series of periodic cataclysms, or as part of a single evolutionary scheme.

But growth and development do not represent the only aspect under which the history of the human race presented itself to the Greeks. There are two lines of tradition, sometimes considered to be diametrically opposed. The one speaks of the gradual improvement of life and its institutions from primitive and brutish beginnings. The other is the tradition of a Golden Age in the past, in comparison with which our present lot is hard and our character sadly degenerate. When we look at them more closely, however, we shall find that the contrast is not a simple one of black and white, and that it was even possible for the two views to be in a measure combined. Let us take the idea of a Golden Age first, and then return to the evolutionary or progressive theories.

We are all familiar with the idea of a period of blissful happiness in the past, whether we take it from the Biblical Garden of Eden or from the poetry and myths of other countries. In these stories the bountifulness of external nature, which lavishes its fruits without any toil on the part of the human race, is usually combined with innocence and mutual love in mankind itself. A life of ease and plenty goes with peaceful thoughts and harmless amusements. Consequently, although the loss of this paradise may sometimes be put down to the jealousy of an anthropomorphic god—a notion that appears in Hesiod and is not altogether absent from the old Hebrew story—it is most commonly attributed to man's own wickedness or folly. In one form or another, the Golden Age or the Garden of Eden will never cease to haunt our imagination. We may abandon it as history, but as a parable of human nature its essential truth remains. To the fancy of poets it has always made a special appeal, sometimes coupled with the wistful hope that it may return and give us back what we have lost. Among the Greeks, it is true, in spite of their readiness to regard the passage of time as circular, this hope was never strong. Their literature indeed is dyed with a curiously persistent tinge of pessimism. The hope has been emphasized rather by others who, taking their cue from the Greek Golden Age or Age of Kronos, have enlisted the possibility of its return in support of current religious, or even political, ideas of a millennium. In the reign of Augustus, it became a commonplace among Roman poets to flatter him as the restorer of the Golden Age. Milton linked it to the Messianic hope, and for him it is the birth of Christ which holds out the promise that 'Time will run back and fetch the Age of Gold'.[8]

Our subject is the Greeks, and about them it is necessary to be a little more precise. No doubt the idea of a lost age of happiness is a very old bit of folklore—borrowed, some would say, from Eastern lands—but the first extant writer to associate it with the epithet 'golden' is Hesiod, and on him most if not all the others depend. Nor does he apply the word to the age, but to the men themselves. Just as we speak of silence as golden, or of a golden opportunity, so in Greece too the word was in common metaphorical use to denote whatever was best of its kind. 'First of all, the gods made a golden race of men' are Hesiod's words, and Plato borrowed his phraseology to describe the three natural classes into which, by what he called a 'high-minded fiction', he divided the men of his ideal state. The best of them were given an admizture of gold in their composition, the next best of silver, while the ordinary run of men contained bronze and iron. So in Hesiod the golden race had been followed by one of silver, 'much worse, neither in stature nor in mind like to the golden'. Then came the race of bronze, cruel and violent, and lastly (if we may omit the race of heroes inserted here out of deference to the authority of Homer) the race of iron to which the poet himself belongs. It is a race condemned to weariness and pain, among whom wickedness flourishes and religion is neglected.[9]

'Gold,' then, refers to the quality of the men. The bygone age in which they lived was called, both by Hesiod and others, the reign of Kronos. In Greek myth Kronos was the father of Zeus, the present ruler of gods and men, who had deposed him and usurped his power. He is the god whom the Romans identified with their native Saturn, so that the happy age of Kronos becomes in Roman poetry *Saturnia regna*. In his time, runs Hesiod's story, men lived like gods except that they were mortal. Pain was unknown, death came like sleep, and the earth bore her fruits in plenty without human toil. After death the men of this race became good spirits, keeping watch over those who followed them.

It is a countryman's paradise that Hesiod—who was himself a farmer—sighs for, in which 'the work of oxen and patient mules would come to an end'. But as it is, Zeus, son of Kronos, has made the means of livelihood hard to find, in his anger at being tricked by Prometheus. Such a myth was not hard for the philosophers to restate in their own terms, with which we are now familiar, of the decreasing powers of the earth as it gets older. So in Lucretius the statement that 'the earth is so broken and worn-out that she can scarcely generate small animals, she who once generated all kinds and gave birth to the huge bodies of wild beasts' leads naturally on to a Hesiodic picture of the old ploughman shaking his head as he sees his labour brought to nought:

> He compares the present with past ages, and often lauds the fortunes of his father. So too the glum planter of withered vines blames the trend of the times, chides the age, and grumbles at the way in which the pious men of old lived an easy life within a narrow plot. He does not grasp that all things gradually decay and pass to the grave, wearied by the long spell of life.[10]

In general, the keynote of the age of Kronos is not wealth and luxury, but a sufficiency of natural food in conjunction with high moral character and a complete absence of wars and dissension. Ease and happiness are linked to simplicity and innocence of mind. So for instance Plato tells us in the *Laws* and the *Politicus*. In these works he has for his own purposes made some remarkable additions to the common stock of myth, but the description of the mode of life of these early men is the traditional one. According to him, the reason why all went so well for men under Kronos is that he knew they were not naturally good or wise enough to be trusted with their own destiny. Left in sole control they would inevitably turn (as they do now) to quarrelling and injustice; and so, just as now man takes care of the inferior animals—goats, oxen and so on —at that time Kronos in his wisdom appointed gods or spirits to take care of men. It looks rather as if the golden race of Hesiod, who became guardian spirits after their death, had been promoted to this status altogether. Under their guiding care, men were kept peaceful, unselfish, law-abiding and just. There was no private property, political organization was unnecessary, and war unknown. Plato adds the usual picture of beneficent nature: 'they had fruit in abundance from trees and other plants, not cultivated by farming, for the earth produced them of her own accord. For the most part they lived in the open air without clothes or bedding, since the seasons were tempered mildly for them and grass springing thickly from the earth provided a soft couch.'[11]

It is worth noticing the extreme simplicity of life in the golden age of Kronos. That men lived at first 'without clothes or bedding' is something that we shall find repeated when we come to consider what we may call the realist school of Greek prehistorians. Take away the unnatural mildness of the climate and the same fact can be adduced as evidence not of the happiness but of the misery of early man. In Plato's account however simplicity, and in particular the absence of private wealth, is counted among the prerequisites of happiness. So far as we know, it was left to the Roman poets to make ironical play with the two senses, literal and metaphorical, of the word 'golden', pointing out that the discovery and use of gold was a characteristic of the degenerate iron age, and was indeed a major factor in the destruction of earlier happiness; but most serious thinkers of Greece would have agreed. Fairy-tales about rivers of gold and jewels growing on trees no doubt existed among the Greeks before they were ridiculed by Lucretius, but the dominant picture is different. From the comic poet Aristophanes we know that in popular speech to say of anyone that he seemed to be living in the age of Kronos did not imply that he was rich, prosperous and happy, but rather that he was old-fashioned even to the point of foolishness.[12]

We have already seen Empedocles to be a thinker of exceptional originality, and it is no surprise to find that he turned the Golden Age idea to his own use and fitted it into his complicated system of cosmogony. The forces of Love and Strife, which in that system control the universe alternately, have a character not only physical but moral. We saw in an earlier chapter how in our present world Strife is undoing the work of Love. The physical meaning of this was that the elements, formerly fused together, are gradually breaking apart. This is the process which has brought about the creation of earth, sea and sky and all manner of creatures including man. Just as the universe had its age of love when all the elements were united, so too in the human sphere the earliest age of man was an age of love in comparison with the present time, for the influence of Strife has been growing continually. Empedocles modifies the familiar succession of the ages by saying that this age of love preceded even the reign of Kronos. As once in the universe at large, so in men's hearts love was the ruling passion, and in particular (since for Empedocles as for the Pythagoreans this was the crux of human behaviour) they had not yet learned to shed blood and eat flesh. In consequence all beasts and birds were tame and friendly to man. Two lines which say that the trees kept their leaves and fruit the whole year round, producing the fruit without stint, may be thought of as descriptive of the same period and so reproducing another feature of the traditional picture of a Golden Age. In exalting especially the moral standard of the first age of mankind, he was in no way departing from the accepted view. A quotation from his poem on this subject, which we owe to the Neoplatonist Porphyry's treatise on vegetarianism, may be translated something like this:

Nor was the war-god worshipped among them nor the battle-cry, nor was Zeus their king nor Kronos nor Poseidon, but the Cyprian [Aphrodite] was queen. Her they propitiated with pious offerings, painted figures and variously scented unguents, sacrifices of unmixed myrrh and fragrant incense, and they poured on the ground libations of yellow honey. But no altar was wet with the shameful slaughter of bulls; nay it was held the foulest defilement to tear out the life and devour the goodly limbs.[13]

Leaving the world of poetry and creative imagination (in which

we may certainly include Plato in some of his moods), let us turn
to the sober, scientific prose of a follower of Aristotle. The Peripatetic Dicaearchus in the 4th century B.C. offered a most interesting account of early man, in which he accepted from poetry and
mythology the idea of an original golden race of good and happy
beings, but rationalized it severely, and in the process laid great
stress on the simplicity and even ignorance in which they lived. It
is summarized for us by Porphyry, who found in it, as in the religious poetry of Empedocles, excellent propaganda for his crusade
against the eating of meat. This is what he says.[14] Dicaearchus,
writing of the life led by the earliest inhabitants of Greece, described them as naturally good and living the best sort of life. Compared with his own contemporaries they were indeed to be
reckoned a golden race, as the poets called them. They ate no
meat, because (and here he quotes Hesiod) the soil gave them all
they wanted of its own accord.[15] Dicaearchus followed the poets
also in setting such a life in the time of Kronos. We have, says
Porphyry, to suppose him to be speaking of what actually happened, and so dismiss the obvious mythical elements, and explain
it by natural causes. Everything grew of its own accord, said the
poet, without the aid of man: yes, of course, for the men themselves
could do nothing to help, since they had not yet learned the art of
agriculture or indeed any other art at all.

To break off from Porphyry's narrative for a moment, presumably Dicaearchus's argument was that, since the first men could
not have learned all at once the secrets of agriculture, the very fact
that they survived is testimony to the essential truth of the poet's
assertion that nature was on their side. But we may notice incidentally that his rationalism did not go far enough for Lucretius. As a
Peripatetic and pupil of Aristotle Dicaearchus was a teleologist,
whereas Lucretius the Epicurean was at pains to deny any tendency
of nature to co-operate with man. After pointing out that half the
world is uninhabitable anyway by reason of mountains, forests,
water, torrid heat or ice, he goes on:

Even the land that remains, nature left to herself would cover
with thorns, were she not resisted by human force, which is

accustomed for its very life to groan over the strong fork and press on the plough to cleave the earth. If we did not turn the fertile sods with the share, and break up the earth's surface to bring them to birth, the crops could never spring up into the clear air of their own accord.[16]

To return to Dicaearchus, he went on to say that the same con- sideration (that is, their lack of skill in husbandry and other arts) explains the poet's contention that the earliest men lived (as we might say) like the lilies of Scripture: they toiled not, neither did they spin. The explanation has a certain disarming simplicity. How could they? They hadn't learned how to. There was also according to the poetic tradition no disease among them. Quite right, says Dicaearchus. This accords with the best medical opinion, which teaches that there is no surer guarantee of health than to keep the body free from the impurities induced by exces- sive or over-rich food. The food available to these men was neither too strong for their stomachs nor available in too great a quantity, but light and scanty. The absence of war and faction is also easy to explain—and here he is in agreement with Plato—for there were no prizes worth fighting for. In sum, the necessary simplicity of their life ensured leisure, a sufficiency of the necessities of life, health, peace and friendship. It is not surprising, he added, that later generations, with their swollen appetites and all the troubles that have attended the complication of existence, looked back to such a life with a kind of longing.

From this beginning, as Porphyry tells us very briefly, Dicaear- chus went on to trace the subsequent stages of human development. The next was the pastoral. It was forced on men's attention that some animals were dangerous and others harmless, and they learned to attack the one sort and make use of the other. The domestication of animals introduced the notion of property. Here were possessions worth having. It was not long before some men began to covet those of others, and so fighting and war began. Then as time went on and men continued to master what appeared to them the most useful arts, they entered the third, or agricultural, stage of life.

Here Porphyry breaks off his summary of what he calls 'Dicaearchus's narration of the blessed life of the earliest Greeks', and returns to his main topic of the eating of meat as the root of all evil including war. Dicaearchus has obviously tried to present a sober, reasoned account and avoid all taint of myth, yet the whole thing is in fact a justification of Hesiod's depiction of the golden race, and his reasoning cannot be said to be very convincing. From the fact that the art of agriculture was unknown, he infers, not that the first men must have had a hard time to keep alive, but that the earth must have produced food for them more easily than it does now. As to their peaceable habits, it does not occur to him (nor did it apparently to Plato) that for men living at a bare subsistence level a morsel of food might be a prize as well worth fighting for as a gold-mine or an oil-well is today. Fanciful as it is, the general line of thought which he pursues has had a remarkably long career. Rousseau, in his discourse on the origin of inequality, blamed agriculture and metallurgy for putting an end to the happy state in which man was before he discovered them.[17] He saw the origin of private property in the acquisition not, like Dicaearchus, of cattle, but of land. Burke in his *Vindication of Natural Society* admitted that 'in the state of nature mankind was subject to many and great inconveniences'; but nevertheless, he thought, 'every endeavour which the art and policy of mankind has used from the beginning of the world to this day, to alleviate and cure them [*sc.* the evils which the Creator has mixed in our cup], have only seemed to introduce new mischiefs, or to aggravate and inflame the old'. Undoubtedly the myth has great value if taken as symbolic of a moral truth—that truth which Epicurus perceived when he said that to make a man rich it is better to diminish his desires than to add to his wealth;[18] but as a historical reconstruction it is difficult to defend.

The interest of Dicaearchus's version is that it shows the conception of the Golden Age stretched almost to breaking point in an endeavour to accommodate what was an essentially romantic and poetic view of the state of early man to the more realistic theories about it which were already current among serious thinkers, and which taught, if they were honestly accepted, a very different lesson. The fact that our first ancestors were helpless, ignorant and unskilled leads naturally to the conclusion not that their life was idyllically happy, but rather that it was uncomfortable and wretched; and this conclusion was an accepted part of Greek tradition at least as early as Aeschylus. This is the view that Lucretius took from Epicurus; and we may notice that, a little inconsistently perhaps, he does not deny that at the beginning of human life the earth bore 'bigger fruits and more of them' (*plura etiam maiora*). After all, it was then 'the flowery springtime of the world' (*novitas tum florida mundi*), and as we have seen, the best contemporary scientific opinion agreed that the earth's fertility had declined through the ages. He also admits that men themselves were stronger and hardier; and although they died in agonies from the attacks of wild beasts, without shelter or medical skill, at least there were no holocausts of thousands in a single day, as happens now in battle. Nevertheless this did not mean (as it might have for Dicaearchus) that far fewer of them died than die nowadays, but only that '*not many more* left the sweet light of life'. In general he seems, quite understandably, to regard these as minor points, and leaves no doubt that for him the evolution of human life has been a progress towards better things.[19]

Stripped of what are really illogical accretions due to the influence of the Golden Age myth, the description in Dicaearchus becomes what we find it in Diodorus, a straightforward picture of want, discomfort and danger. This is how Diodorus puts it, following as we shall see much earlier writers:

> They say that the first men lived in an unorganized and beast-like condition, going out separately to find their food and gathering the most appetizing plants and the fruit that grew without cultivation on the trees. Warred on by wild animals, expedience taught them to help each other, and herded together by fear they gradually became aware of each others' characters.

There follows a sentence about the beginning of language, and he continues:

> Thus the first men, since nothing useful for life had yet been discovered, led a toilsome existence, bare of clothing, unused

to house or fire, and altogether ignorant of cultivated food. Not knowing how to harvest the wild food, they made no store of fruits against times of want. Hence many of them died in the winter from cold and famine.[20]

The theories that we have looked at so far should warn us against attempting any all-embracing generalization about the Greek outlook on life. Were they optimistic believers in progress, or pessimists who saw in human history only a steady decline from higher standards? Undoubtedly the dream of a past Golden Age had very widespread currency, and fits with a characteristic strain of general pessimism. From Hesiod's complaint that life among this race of iron is insupportable we go on to the cry of the chorus in Sophocles's *Oedipus at Colonus* that it were better not to be born, and once born the best that a man can hope for is to die as soon as possible—no isolated outburst occasioned by the particular tragedy of the House of Laius, for it is echoed in places as diverse as Theognis and the fragment of a lost dialogue by Aristotle.[21]

The cyclic view of history is also often quoted as conducive to pessimism, and when it was extended into detail, then to our mind at least its 'endless monotonous iteration', as J. B. Bury called it, does have a depressing effect. Even the general idea that the universe will again dissolve into its elements, or that mankind is destined to be almost wiped out in some future flood or conflagration, is cited as putting a stop to any hopes of indefinite progress. As to that, we may say first of all that this was no imminent threat. Today we may be appalled by the possibility of self-destruction in an atomic war, but the Greeks were spared that horror, What they looked forward to corresponds rather in modern terms to a future ice-age or the eventual cooling of the sun; and neither of these does much to curb our enjoyment of life or our zest for progress. Secondly, some cyclic theories at least held out the hope that if we were now on the downward grade, the wheel would turn again and the Golden Age was not only in the past but in the future as well. According to the strange myth in which Plato expresses cyclic change in his *Politicus*, the Creator, when he first made the universe, himself imparted its rotation and kept it under his guidance. At the end of an era, however, he released his control, and left to itself it began to revolve in the opposite direction. In this era, with God's hand removed, everything within it begins to deteriorate, and so continues until God—since its complete destruction is no part of the divine plan—takes control and reverses the direction once more.[22]

What impressed Aristotle, the most scientific spirit of antiquity, about the recurrent catastrophes in which he believed, was the loss that they entailed of the accumulated wisdom and knowledge of the ages. Yet the prospect of a repetition of this loss did not discourage nor prevent him from looking on the advancement of philosophy and science as the best and highest, as well as the most enjoyable of human pursuits. Side by side with cyclic theories, and undiminished by the poets' lament of man's decline from an age of gold to one of iron, we may read in Greek literature paeans of praise for the ingenuity of man, his increasing knowledge, and even—though this never assumed in ancient Greece the importance which it has today—his growing command over nature.

These ideas of progress we shall look at more closely in the next chapter. If in closing this one I may venture a personal opinion, I should say that the Greeks were neither wholly optimistic nor wholly pessimistic in their outlook. To a mature and thoughtful people, such as they were, human nature appears neither as wholly degenerate nor in every way improving, but as an enigma, the answer to which must be sought in religion rather than in philosophy or science alone. What impressed them was the paradox, at no time more apparent than at the present day, that a race so gifted with intelligence and capable of such miraculous advancement in the understanding and subjugation of external nature, can yet be so utterly foolish and wicked in mutual relations and the management of its own affairs: unimaginable intellectual progress goes hand in hand with moral imbecility. This the Greeks saw, and it brings them at times very close to us. It is summed up in another chorus of Sophocles: All devices are man's and never does the future find him at a loss. Of subtlety passing belief are the achievements of his skill, and they lead him at times to good, but at times to evil.[23]

5

The Idea of Progress

Usus et impigrae simul experientia mentis
paulatim docuit pedetemptim progredientes.

LUCRETIUS 5. 1452-3

The first and greatest of Greek poets, Homer, has so far only received a passing mention in these pages, and this perhaps calls for apology. It is easy to reply that he was no philosopher or political theorist, and had little to say about the origins either of life or of human institutions. But the Greek attitude to the *Iliad* and the *Odyssey* was different from ours. Where we see only two magnificent epic poems, in which the didactic element is at a minimum, they looked for instruction on an astonishing variety of subjects, from religion to military science or even boatbuilding. Consequently whatever the poet's own intentions may have been, his words are likely to have had a disproportionate influence on later writers.

Behind the fairy-tale of the Cyclopes in the *Odyssey*, as Mr Moses Finley has said, 'there lay a distinct view of social evolution'. The Cyclopes were a race of powerful and cruel beings, 'more like mountain-crags than mortal men'. They had no laws, nor did they meet for counsel, but lived apart, each in a mountain cave with his own wives and children, ruling over these but paying no attention to his fellows. Polyphemus, mightiest of them all, into whose cave Odysseus and his companions had so rashly entered, called Odysseus a fool for claiming mercy in the name of Zeus the god of strangers: 'We pay no heed to Zeus or the other blessed gods, for we are much the stronger.' In the externals of their life these immoral beings enjoyed many of the simple blessings of the Golden Age. 'Overbearing and lawless, they put their trust in the immortal gods and neither sow nor plough. Everything grows without cultivation—wheat, barley and vines—and rain from Zeus gives them increase.' They lived a purely rural existence, herding sheep and goats, and without any technical arts such as shipbuilding.[1]

A fairy-tale indeed, and yet as I have said, it was the habit of the Greeks to take their Homer seriously. So we find Plato in his account of the evolution of society citing the Cyclopes as represen-tative of a certain early stage of development which, he says, may still be found among both Greeks and foreign peoples. He quotes the lines about their solitary life without laws or common council. Another speaker replies, 'Homer seems to bear out your theory when in mythological form he connects their primitive state with savagery'. 'He does,' says the other, 'and we may take him as our witness that such an order of society in fact occurs from time to time.' For a later stage, the building of cities, Plato again takes Homer as his authority, quoting the lines from the *Iliad* about the founding of Dardania by Dardanus: 'for not yet had holy Ilium been built in the plain to be a city of human kind, but they still dwelt on the slopes of many-fountained Ida'.[2]

So far, then, as the Cyclopes of the *Odyssey* contributed to the Greek view of early man, it was an influence in the direction of separating the two elements of a past Golden Age: easy living and kindly, peaceful character. Earth bore her fruits without their labour, yet they were lawless, selfish, cruel, and certainly not vegetarians, as Odysseus and his companions learned to their cost. Other passing touches in Homer—the easy life of the Libyans, the gardens of Alcinous and the close relationship of his people to the gods, or the miraculous climate of the Elysian plain and of Olympus itself—were pressed into service by later writers who wanted to describe a Golden Age in the past. But it was not Homer's concern to do this. All that we may say in general is that, by stamping on Greek minds the idea of a heroic age in the past, his effect must have been to incline them to a theory of degeneracy

F   [81]

rather than progress. It was of course a degeneracy particularly in physical prowess and valour. These were the qualities that distinguished the Homeric heroes, and it is the loss of these that the poet laments in the sad phrase οἷοι νῦν βροτοί εἰσιν—'as men are now'—with which he contrasts the mighty deeds of his heroes with the feebleness of his own generation.[3]

The first known Greek to crystallize in an explicit phrase the idea of progress is the poet-theologian Xenophanes, the bitter opponent of Homer and Hesiod, at the end of the 6th or early in the 5th century B.C. We have two lines of his which run:

> The gods did not reveal to men all things in the beginning,
> but in course of time, by searching, they find out better.

Xenophanes was a religious-minded man and no doubt did not mean to deny the guidance of heaven in human affairs; but in these lines he speaks unequivocally of man's own efforts and powers of invention as leading him to better things. Next in time we come to Aeschylus, who gives the credit for human progress to the culture-hero Prometheus; yet it is not an easy question to decide how far, in this border-time between myth and reason, the poet knew that he was using mythological terms to describe a natural and purely human process. First let us see how he describes the progress itself. Prometheus, chained to a rock by the tyrant Zeus for his 'man-loving ways', recounts to the daughters of Oceanus first of all the sorry state of primitive man, and then the benefits which they have derived from his teaching. The gift above all gifts, namely fire, the bestowal of which had especially aroused the wrath of Zeus, has been mentioned earlier, and described as 'the teacher of all arts, the great resource'.[4]

I will just allow myself one preliminary observation. Prometheus is an ancient and fully personalized mythological character, prominent already in Hesiod, yet his name is one of transparent meaning. It is a regularly-formed Greek word, and means the Forethinker (or perhaps even Forethought in the abstract). This is emphasized early in the play, when Zeus's minion taunts the fettered Titan on the inappropriateness of his name: 'Falsely do the gods call thee Forethinker (Forethought?), for thou art thyself in need of a forethinker' (or 'of forethought'). Throughout his speech, therefore, we may keep in mind that, to a Greek ear, he is recounting the benefits that men owe to Forethought. Moreover the first thing he says is that formerly they were witless creatures, and that what he did was to teach them to use their own minds. Aided by Prometheus, or the God of forethought, they achieved advancement by the exercise of their own intelligence. [5]

First of all, he claims, they had eyes and ears but saw and heard to no purpose. Lost in confusion they enjoyed no genuine life. They had no houses, for they lacked the skill of carpentry, but lived underground like ants, in the dim recesses of caves. They acted at random, with no sure sign of spring or harvest-time or winter, until I, Forethought, revealed to them the risings and settings of the stars. I also taught them to reckon with numbers, to write, to yoke oxen and use their labour, to harness horses and to sail the seas. I showed them the use of medicinal herbs, and revealed the secrets of prophecy and the taking of omens. None but I discovered for them those aids to human life that are hidden in the ground—the metals copper, iron, silver and gold. The speech ends with the impressive sentence: 'In one short phrase you may know everything: all arts, all skill, men owe to the Forethinker.'

How hard it is to enter fully into the minds of men to whom personification comes so naturally as it did to the Greeks! If the spirit of Forethought—Prometheus—is not a living, divine person, suffering torments for having defied the tyranny of Zeus, the whole tragedy has no significance. Yet I find it difficult to believe that in writing this speech Aeschylus had no thought of the meaning of the word, no consciousness that he was really describing a technical revolution brought about historically by human ingenuity alone. At least we are not far off in time from the wonderful chorus in Sophocles in which the marvels of technical progress— from speech to agriculture, sailing, housing, medicine and many others—are cited as evidence of the surpassing intelligence and indomitable will of man himself; [6] and we shall soon come to a work of exceptional interest in which a modified version of the Prometheus story is used intentionally and explicitly as an allegory of the natural advancement of civilization by human endeavour acting under the pressure of necessity.

By the middle of the 5th century we find scattered hints that a rationalistic view of man's development was being taught by the natural philosophers. Anaxagoras said that whereas the animals are our masters in strength and speed, our superiority in memory, in learning from experience, and in cleverness enables us to make use of them and their products, milking the cow, appropriating honey from the bee, and so forth. Taking a different point of view, but still emphasizing the powers of human reason, Democritus held that we learned our techniques from the animals themselves. In weaving we are pupils of the spider, in house-building of the swallow, in singing of the swan and the nightingale. One of the greatest of all 5th-century rationalists was Protagoras, famous in particular for two pronouncements: first that all truth is relative to the experience of the individual, and second, a confession of religious agnosticism: 'I have no means of knowing whether gods exist or not.' This impressive figure takes the centre of the stage in one of Plato's dialogues, and the account of the origins of human society which is there put into his mouth is worth considering in full.[7]

The question at issue in the dialogue is the nature of a moral quality—in Greek *arete*—which may roughly be rendered as civic virtue. It is that in men which makes it possible for organized societies to exist, and when possessed to an outstanding degree raises the individual to be a successful statesman. Is it a natural gift, innate in all of us to some extent, or are men naturally solitary and anti-social, and only brought to live together by bitter experience or by teaching from others who have the gift already? Protagoras offers to give his views either in the form of reasoned argument, or as a story. His audience leaves the choice to him, and he decides on the narrative form as being the more entertaining. This is important. We know from the start that the story is an allegory, in part indeed a genetic account where a static analysis of human nature would have been equally suitable. Even apart from Protagoras's open avowal, his well-known scepticism would warn us that when he brings the gods into his tale they can be thought away as deliberate mythical trappings. This is the story.[8]

Once upon a time, there existed gods but no mortal creatures. When the appointed time came for these also to be born, the gods formed them within the earth out of a mixture of earth and fire and the substances which are compounded of earth and fire.

We recognize the familiar idea that the first animals were formed within the earth. Their substance is a mixture of the four elements, as had been taught by Empedocles. Plato uses similar language in the *Timaeus*, where he describes in detail, and again with a fully conscious use of mythical imagery, the nature of the universe and man. To make the human race, the lesser gods entrusted with this task 'borrowed from the universe portions of fire and earth, water and air, on promise of repayment'—a reminder that as our bodies are composed of the elements, so to the elements they will return again. At our death the cosmos receives back its own.

And when they were ready to bring them to the light, they charged Prometheus and Epimetheus with the task of equipping them and allotting suitable powers to each kind.

Epimetheus, who figures in Hesiod, is the brother of Prometheus and his antithesis. He stands for simple-mindedness and foolishness, as his name indicates ('Afterthought' or 'Afterthinker').

Now Epimetheus begged Promethus to allow him to do the distribution himself—'and when I have done it', he said, 'you can review it'. So he persuaded him and set to work. In his allotment he gave to some creatures strength without speed, and equipped the weaker kinds with speed. Some he armed with weapons, while to the unarmed he gave some other faculty and so contrived means for their preservation. To those that he endowed with smallness, he granted winged flight or a dwelling underground; to those which he increased in stature, their size itself was a protection. Thus he made his whole distribution on a principle of compensation, being careful by these devices that no species should be destroyed. When he had sufficiently provided means of escape from mutual slaughter, he contrived their comfort against the seasons sent from Zeus, clothing them with thick hair or hard skins sufficient to ward off the winter's cold,

[85]

and effective also against heat; and he planned that when they went to bed, the same coverings should serve as proper and natural bedclothes for each species. He shod them also, some with hooves, others with hard and bloodless skin.

Next he appointed different sorts of food for them; to some the grass of the earth, to others the fruit of trees, to others roots. Some he allowed to gain their nourishment by devouring other animals, and these he made less prolific, while he bestowed fertility on their victims, and so preserved the species.

I am no biologist, but I imagine that when we think away, as Protagoras has given us licence to do, the transparently mythological figure of Epimetheus, we are left here with a very good description of the way in which the balance between species is in fact preserved by variety in the distribution of natural endowments —or as Protagoras puts it, 'on a principle of compensation'. It illustrates also the truth that nature's devices for preservation seem to operate only at species level and to ignore the individual, as with those animals that are a natural prey to others but exceptionally prolific.

Now Epimetheus was not a particularly clever person, and before he realized it he had used up all the available powers on the brute beasts, and being left with the human race on his hands unprovided for, did not know what to do with them. While he was puzzling about this, Prometheus came to inspect the work, and found the other animals well off for everything, but man naked, unshod, unbedded, and unarmed: and already the appointed day had come when man too was to emerge from within the earth into the daylight. Prometheus therefore, being at a loss to provide any other means of salvation for man, stole from Hephaestus and Athena the gift of skill in the crafts, together with fire—for without fire it was impossible for anyone to possess or use this skill—and bestowed it on man. In this way man acquired sufficient resources to keep himself alive, but had no political wisdom. This was in the keeping of Zeus.

This passage shows once again how, to an age before evolution

THE IDEA OF PROGRESS

in the modern sense had been thought of, one of the most puzzling
things about the human race was how it could ever have survived
in the first place. Now it is protected by devices for shelter and defence which men themselves have invented. But before these
existed, how could a species so ill-provided by nature with the
means of preservation have stood up to the rigours of climate and
the attacks of wild beasts? The question excited Greek philosophers from the days of Anaximander.

At this stage then, says Protagoras summing up, men had first
of all religion, for they were in a special relationship to the gods
and believed in them from the start: also, by the arts which
Prometheus had bestowed on them, they were quickly able to
communicate with one another by speech, to make houses,
clothes and bedding, and to obtain food from the earth. He continues:

Thus provided for, they lived at first in scattered groups; there
were no cities. Consequently they were devoured by wild beasts,
since they were in every respect the weaker, and their technical
skill, though a sufficient aid to their nurture, did not extend to
making war on the beasts, for they had not the art of politics, of
which the art of war is a part. They sought therefore to save
themselves by coming together and founding fortified cities, but
when they gathered in communities they injured one another
for want of political skill, and so scattered again and continued
to be devoured. Zeus, therefore, fearing the total destruction of
our race, sent Hermes to impart to men the qualities of respect
for others and a sense of justice, so as to bring order into our
cities and create a bond of friendship and union. Hermes asked
Zeus in what manner he was to bestow these gifts on men. 'Shall
I distribute them as the arts were distributed—that is, on the
principle that one trained doctor suffices for many laymen, and
so with the other experts? Shall I distribute justice and respect
for their fellows in this way, or to all alike?' 'To all', said Zeus.
'Let all have their share. There could never be cities if only a
few shared in these virtues, as in the arts. Moreover, you must
lay it down as my law that if anyone is incapable of acquiring

his share of these two virtues he shall be put to death as a plague to the city.'

What Protagoras seems to have done in this story is to construct, partly at least from existing 5th-century Ionian philosophy, a rationalistic account of the origin of animal and human life, and of human civilization, and graft on to it the tale of Prometheus and Epimetheus, which not unnaturally has undergone some modification in the process. When we take away the gods whom Protagoras has introduced into his tale to make it, as he has said himself, 'more pleasing', we are left with an account of human development remarkably like that which I quoted from Diodorus in the last chapter, many features of which may be with good reason referred to that period and tradition.[9] With the mythological embroidery removed, the significance of the account is this.

Protagoras regards technical ability, including the use of fire and —implicitly at least—of tools, as belonging to man in his earliest and most primitive condition; for in mythical terms they were bestowed by Prometheus, just as wings, fur, hooves, etc. were bestowed on the lower animals by Epimetheus, before they even emerged from the earth into the light of day. No doubt Protagoras regarded them as stemming directly from the possession of reason, the faculty which in Greek eyes marked the essential distinction between men and beasts, and which in Aeschylus's version of the myth was the first gift of the Fire-bringer.

Armed with these faculties, man starts his life on earth, and the first thing he does is to institute religious worship. This is explained as due to his 'share in the divine', a universal article of Greek belief connected in particular with his possession of reason. Here the phrase has a double significance. In terms of the myth, man shared in a divine dispensation because it was the gift of a divine being, Prometheus. But this gift was the gift of reason, which alone could enable him to develop the arts and crafts, and to share in reason is to share in the gods' own portion.[10] The fact that man has it is one proof of his kinship with them. As to Protagoras's own position, he probably recognized worship as something specifically and universally human, but put aside as unanswerable the question of the existence and nature of its object. Belief in the existence of gods probably appeared to him to be a conclusion drawn from the universal diffusion of their worship, and this conclusion did not seem to him a necessary one.[11]

It is interesting to notice that religion, the awareness of the numinous, is taken to be a primitive phenomenon, preceding the acquisition of moral sense, yet without any mention of the common explanation of it as having originated either out of awe at the majestic and regular movements of the heavenly bodies or from the fear caused by meteorological events like thunder and lightning. Technical ability, then, and worship of the gods were present in man from the beginning. Moral and social virtues, however, were not. They were acquired later, after bitter experience of the fatal results of an inability to combine. Protagoras's answer to the old question how early man survived, in spite of his disabilities in comparison with other species, is that in fact large numbers of men did not. Even their technical cleverness was not enough to preserve them, and the whole race would have died out had not the social virtues been developed. To defeat the beasts called for communal effort, and this in turn demanded such qualities as altruism and justice. The rule of 'every man for himself' was leading to extinction. On the one hand, then, these moral virtues are not, like reason, an essential and original mark of distinction between man and the lower animals, but an acquired characteristic. On the other hand, once acquired, their presence in some degree became universal, or practically so, since continued human existence would be impossible without them. They are not, says Zeus in the myth, to be distributed on the same principle as the arts. We cannot have a world in which some men alone are morally endowed as some have a talent for medicine, others for music and so forth.

In this theory of human nature we have Protagoras's explanation of the antecedent possibility of social and political organization, the foundation on which, in his view, must be built any theory of government, of the purpose and effects of punishment, and many other matters of equally universal importance. It is well thought out and subtly expressed, and an effort to understand it will be worth while. This calls for a careful consideration both of the myth and of the explanation with which, in the dialogue, Protagoras follows it up.

A central topic of discussion in the second half of the 5th century was whether virtue (*arete*) was 'by nature'—that is, a natural and universal human faculty like sight or hearing, though doubtless capable, like them, of being improved or atrophied—or rather something which must be acquired by instruction or correction or otherwise, in other words an artificial adjunct to our human nature. To maintain his position vis-à-vis Socrates in the dialogue, Protagoras had to defend simultaneously two positions which were not easy to reconcile. First, virtue is not a natural endowment of the human race, but one which is acquired and cultivated by training. After all, he earned his living as a professional Sophist by offering to teach *arete* for a fee, so that nothing less than his whole livelihood was at stake in the question whether or not it could be imparted by teaching. His second and more difficult thesis was that, in spite of this, as men live at present no one is entirely devoid of this quality. All have a share of it, though not necessarily an equal share. What made this second point necessary was that he had undertaken to justify the principle underlying Athenian democracy. It rested, Socrates had said, on the assumption that in technical matters like shipbuilding or architecture, which can only be mastered by training, only the expert in that particular art is to be trusted, whereas in matters of public policy one man's opinion was as good as another's. But if the common man's opinion is to be trusted here, then political sense (which is an important part of *arete*) must, one would suppose, be something innate in everyone and call for no special training.

In the myth, then, we find, first, that the sense of justice and self-restraint were not in men from the beginning, but secondly, that when they were bestowed, they were by Zeus's order to be bestowed on all. This downright statement is however a little weakened when Zeus goes on to say to Hermes that 'if anyone is incapable of acquiring these two virtues', he is to be put to death. The possibility is envisaged, for they are no part of the original nature of man. This is already fixed, and even Zeus cannot alter it.

[90]

How Protagoras fitted this part of his myth to the facts, we see from the more prosaic explanation which follows it. All men living in a community like the city of Athens, he claims, have civic or social virtue in some measure. Those who behave badly have less of it than others, but none is absolutely wicked. If Socrates were ever to meet men completely lacking in *arete*—man who, *ex hypothesi*, would be leading a solitary, brutish life and in any civilized community would be put to death or permanently locked up—he would long for the most villainous men in Athens as being, by comparison, paragons of virtue.

Today, then, everyone has some moral sense. How have they acquired it? Not of course from Heaven: that was part of the story-telling. They have acquired it by teaching, but this fact goes unnoticed because the teaching starts at birth and continues throughout life. From earliest infancy parents and nurse are telling the child what to do and what not to do, and reinforcing their teaching if necessary by forcible correction. At school (and here Protagoras gives a fascinatingly informative description of Athenian education) much more emphasis is laid on moral than on intellectual progress. In adult life the State continues this education through its laws, which prohibit certain actions under pain of punishment, and a man's friends and neighbours all co-operate, by advice or rebuke, since it is to our advantage that our neighbours should behave well. Socrates had objected that if virtue could be taught, it should be possible to point out the teachers of those who excelled in it, great statesmen or others who had deserved especially well of the community. But this, says Protagoras, would be like asking who taught us to speak our native language. We grew up speaking it without any recognized teachers, and yet it was being taught us by everyone all the time. The outstanding excellence of certain individuals is to be explained by exceptional natural aptitude. Of his own profession, he modestly remarks in conclusion that although everyone teaches virtue to some extent, it is only to be expected that some can teach it rather better. That is all that we can ask for, and, he says, as it happens I honestly believe that I am a better teacher than others.

I think this is a fair account of what Protagoras is trying to say, and it saves him from several accusations of inconsistency that have been levelled at him in the past. One however remains. It has been said that he postulates virtue as a pre-condition of social life, but at the same time represents it as a product of social life, resulting from the teaching which everyone receives from earliest childhood through his membership of an already existing civilized society. This objection has been recently discussed by Professor G. B. Kerferd, whose conclusion is: 'Protagoras's answer, if not satisfying, is clear and consistent. Men, before societies existed, were unable to form societies, because they lacked what they could only learn from and through societies. Accordingly, divine intervention was required to enable the process to start.'[12]

If I have understood this rightly, I find it a slightly disappointing conclusion to an article which has thrown much light on the meaning of Protagoras's discourse. It seems to take the myth literally at this point, whereas we know for certain that where the gods were concerned, Protagoras was an agnostic. The intervention of Zeus is part of the symbolism of the myth. If the dilemma could be pointed out to him, I imagine that his answer would be something like this:

'You are always trying to pin me down to a clear-cut logical alternative.' (This is in fact a complaint which he makes to Socrates several times in the course of the dialogue.) 'You are talking in abstractions, but that is not how life works. You say "either virtue is a pre-condition of social life or else it arose out of it when it was already established", and you accuse me of trying to have it both ways. What happened I suppose was something like this. Forced by necessity to unite, men made sporadic attempts to do so in various parts of the world. Where they did not succeed in educating one another sufficiently in the civic virtues, these attempts failed, and those who made them perished. Gradually however, "with necessity itself for their teacher" as one of our Ionian writers has recently put it—was it that clever young man Democritus from my own city? He will go far—they learned from these attempts at social life what was needed if they were to be successful. Only those who did so learn survived. Thus I am quite right in saying both that virtue is not innate as an original part of human nature and at the same time that it is universal among all existing men.'

It is not within the scope or purpose of these lectures to enter the rich field of Greek political theory.[13] This made it seem all the more worth while spending a little time in trying to understand an important conception of human nature, which is after all the raw material of all government, on the treatment of which its success or failure must depend. Protagoras was an outstanding thinker, and the loss of his works is one of the severer blows that time has dealt us. In their absence, much of our appreciation of his quality results from Plato's portrait of him, and this is all the more impressive because Plato was utterly opposed to him on fundamentals, and moreover could not resist the temptation to poke a little fun at his vanity and other harmless foibles. His chief characteristics were an empirical outlook, a preference for knowledge that could be put to practical use, and a sense of moderation. Abstractions were anathema to him, as is illustrated in another field by his criticism of mathematicians for saying that a straight line touches a circle only at a point. This applies to no straight and circular bodies in our experience nor can it ever, however perfectly they may be formed. A hoop does not touch a straight edge at a single point only. Where then is the truth of it to be found?[14]

The same preference for commonsense marks his contribution to the contemporary *nomos-physis* controversy. These words mean respectively custom, or convention, and nature, and the burning question was whether moral laws are a part of the order of nature with an absolute and universal validity, or something secondary and artificial, and relative to the temporary conventions of a particular order of society. If Socrates and Plato were out-and-out defenders of moral absolutes, this was largely because many of those who denied them had tended to go to the opposite practical extreme, and become champions of a state of moral anarchy. In his *Gorgias* Plato depicts Socrates in conversation with one of these, a man who exalts what he calls the life according to nature. This, in his opinion, consists in letting one's desires grow as big as possible and making sure of the means of satisfying them. Selfishness is nature's law, and her just man, as opposed to the just man of convention, is represented by a Sardanapallus, the out-and-out tyrant who lives a life of ease and luxury at the expense of his subjects. A historical exponent of a similar view was the Sophist Antiphon. There were obviously good practical grounds why Socrates and Plato should oppose this outlook on life.

Protagoras also took the view that moral notions like those of justice and altruism were not in nature, but secondary and relative. This seemed to him, on empirical grounds, the most reasonable conclusion. But it did not lead him to proclaim that the state of nature was to be exalted and the moral virtues decried. The reason why man had evolved his codes was simple and sufficient. They were a prerequisite of social life, and man's situation in the world was such that without life in societies he would disappear from the face of the earth. Nature and convention were indeed opposed, but the path to be followed was that of convention rather than nature. Lacking the social virtues, 'when they gathered in communities they injured one another, and so scattered again and continued to be devoured'. This view of the matter implies of course that human nature does contain the *possibility* of advancement in morality. That a certain natural aptitude is involved, and that men may be variously endowed in this respect, is clear both from what Protagoras says in the Platonic dialogue and from a quotation out of his own writings which has come down to us: 'Teaching needs nature as well as practice.' But to bring morality into active existence, to know that it is this side of our nature which must be cultivated rather than the powerful forces within us that tend to rampant individualism—that is the fruit of long experience.

6

What is Man?
The Philosophical Implications

By the classical period of Greek thought the idea of a past
Golden Age had been very widely replaced by the view of
man's early condition as 'brutish' and 'disorderly'. These
words—especially 'brutish' or 'animal-like'—are repeated like an
echo by a number of writers. Critias, who played a notorious part
in the short-lived rule of the Thirty Tyrants at Athens and died
about 403 B.C., wrote a play called *Sisyphus* from which a long
speech has survived beginning: 'There was a time when the life of
men was disorderly, brutish and ruled by force.' The speech is
notable for its atheism, religion being cynically described as the
invention of a clever ruler to ensure men's good behaviour through
fear. A description of early man by the tragic poet Moschion in the
next century begins: 'Once upon a time men lived like the brutes.'
'Brutish' again is the adjective used by Theseus in Euripides's
Supplices, 'disorderly and brutish' is echoed in Diodorus, and
Roman poets like Lucretius followed their Greek masters: the
first men 'vitum tractabant more ferarum'. A feature of primitive
life in this circle of thought was cannibalism. We find it in
Moschion and Diodorus, and one of the things for which
Orpheus was revered in his capacity as a culture-hero was that he
put a stop to this savage practice. This is another link between the
Cyclopes of Homer and Greek beliefs about primitive man in
general.[1]

It is interesting to see this notion of man's early state applied to
their science by Greek medical writers. The Hippocratic treatise

On Ancient Medicine was probably written in the 5th century. Like contemporary writers on the origins of civilization in general, its author ascribes the rise of his own art not to Asclepius or any other god, but to 'necessity'. He uses the same word 'brutish' to describe the crude diet of primitive men. Forced to live on the natural products of the earth like animals, they suffered agonies of indigestion, leading even to death, until they learned to modify the nature of food-plants by cultivation, to balance their diet by judicious mixture, and to mitigate its crudity by the art of cooking. [2]

Moschion's description of primitive life is worth quoting more fully for comparison on the one hand with the naturalistic accounts of Protagoras and Diodorus, and on the other with those of his fellow-playwrights Aeschylus and Euripides. Both of these ostensibly attributed human progress to the intervention of a god, but we saw some reason to think that the notion of divine providence lay like a fairly thin veneer over a fundamentally materialistic and evolutionary view. Moschion is more openly sceptical. At first men lived like animals in mountain caves or glens. They had no houses or cities, no ploughs or iron tools. The gloom of this picture is unrelieved by any of those intrusions from the Golden Age which we have found in similar accounts elsewhere. The earth did not compensate for man's lack of skill by greater natural fertility, indeed her barrenness drove them to cannibalism. Thus Moschion denies the widely held theory that the earth's fertility has steadily declined. Force was the only law, a contrast to the idea of Plato and Dicaearchus that in the beginning, when men were without the arts, war and contention were also unknown. What altered this state of things, says Moschion, was time. Time is 'the begetter and nurturer of all things'. It may have been, he adds (as though the matter were of little importance), Prometheus who taught them better, or it may have been necessity or nature itself through long practice. Then came the cultivation of grain and vines, the taming of oxen and use of the plough. Houses and cities were built and the savagery of life was tamed.

The growth of civilization and morals is here linked with the cultivation of grain, called by Moschion 'holy Demeter's fruit of gentle nurture'. There were two competing Greek answers to the question what was the one all-important discovery that set men on the road from savagery to civilization. In the Prometheus myth it is fire, a reasonable opinion when we try to imagine what life without fire would be like. We should of course still be in the stone age. Fire for Aeschylus is 'the teacher of all arts, the great resource'. Prometheus stole it for men when he wished to give them skill in the crafts, for as Protagoras rightly said, without fire no one can possess or use this skill. Xenophon too describes fire as 'assistant in every art and in all that men contrive for their good', and the same connexion of thought is brought out by a poet in the Homeric Hymn to Hephaestus. There the god of fire is praised as the one who 'with grey-eyed Athena taught men noble works upon the earth, though aforetime they lived like beasts in caves on the mountains'. The learned author of the treatise *On Ancient Medicine* would presumably have agreed, since he attributed the advance of men towards civilization from a 'fierce and brutish' existence in large part to the invention of cooking.[3]

On the other hand we have the claim of agriculture to be the root not only of the arts but of the whole ethos of civilization. This was the lesson in particular of the religion of Demeter. It had its culture-hero too, Triptolemos, whom Demeter sent abroad to take to mankind the gift, not of fire like Prometheus, but of grain and the art of the ploughman. Her cult-title Thesmophoros shows what was in men's minds, for it means 'she who brings law'.

Now the greatest centre of Demeter-worship was the little Attic town of Eleusis, which at an early stage was politically united with Athens. From that time the Athenians regarded themselves as the especial favourites of Demeter, and the claim of agriculture to be the mother of all civilization was promoted in no small degree by Athenian patriotic propaganda. They liked to appear as the standard-bearers of the good life, and one way to do so was to emphasize their especial relation to the goddess of agriculture; for to quote their spokesman Isocrates, the fruits of the field have been the instrument whereby mankind is raised above the life of the beasts.[4] This claim too has its support in fact, for it was after all the discovery of how to till the soil that first turned men from wandering nomads or hunters into members of settled communities having a stake in the land and a permanent home, with all the consequences of law-abidingness and peaceful co-existence that that entails.

Fire and agriculture—Hephaestus and Prometheus on the one hand, Demeter and Triptolemos on the other—are the twin symbols of civilization. Each has its champions, for the claim of each is undeniable, but neither is complete without the other. Prometheus stands for man's technical progress, Triptolemos for his moral development. Both are necessary to a full and civilized existence, but today one may perhaps put in an especial plea for the gentle Demeter and her envoy, if only because Hephaestus and Prometheus, the spirits of the fire and the forge, have in recent years been demanding rather more than their fair share of man's attention.

Setting aside stories of a Golden Age, the theories of the origin and growth of human society and culture which we have so far considered see it as arising under pressure of stern necessity. Aeschylus, Protagoras, Critias, Moschion, the Orphic poet, and the source of Diodorus all agree that man's earliest condition was brutish and pitiable. He lived like the other animals except that he was far less fitted than they to stand up to the rigours of their life. It was also possible, as we saw earlier, for features of the Golden Age, and its accompanying view of human history as a steady degeneration, to be combined in curious ways with the idea of progress from a lower state. A further, and particularly striking, illustration of this attempt to have it both ways is found in a passage from Virgil's *Aeneid* which probably goes back to a Stoic source. It teaches that the Golden Age of Saturn lies indeed in the past, but was not the earliest age of man. Peace and law were imposed by Saturn on an ignorant and rebellious race living a poor, rough life in scattered groups on the mountains. To these he brought the Golden Age, but later a race of baser metal arose and became infected with avarice and war. Diodorus says the same about the age of Kronos: Cretan legend tells that when Kronos became king he converted men from savage to peaceful ways.[5]

When we turn to the greatest of Greek philosophers, Plato and Aristotle, we find that they too present us with evolutionary accounts, but the spirit that informs them is very different. Behind the theories reproduced by Protagoras and in the first book of Diodorus there lies the Ionian tradition of free inquiry motivated by a pure historical curiosity. Even the poets, in and after the age of the Sophists—a Euripides, a Critias or a Moschion—were strongly influenced by this spirit. Euripides in particular was reckoned as a disciple of Anaxagoras. He several times introduces the philosopher's physical theories into his poetry, and praises the student of the 'ageless order of nature'.[6] The writers on whom these poets relied were genuinely interested in the subject for its own sake: they really wanted to know how the first men survived and what was likely to have been their mode of life.

This was not the aim of Plato and Aristotle. Their interest was in their own day, their questions were practical and their outlook teleological. To them the form of primitive society mattered only in so far as a definite view about it might serve the ultimate purpose of deciding on the *best* form of political association. Their approach was in truth not genetic at all, but analytic. They were political theorists trying to understand, and improve, the structure of a contemporary Greek city-state. For this purpose they wanted to reduce it to its simplest elements, and in their view a good method of doing this was to imagine it as being built up historically from a small and simple to a larger and more complex structure. We have seen[7] how Plato used this device in the *Laws*. The genesis of the ideal city in the *Republic* is presented even more schematically and with less parade of historical circumstance. The motive of the inquiry is not historical but philosophical. A question has been raised about the nature of justice. Justice, says Socrates, occurs in communities as well as in individuals, and it may be easier to discover if we imagine[8] a city in the course of its evolution. He continues simply: 'A city arises because none of us is sufficient to himself.' Naturally if a community is pictured at the outset as arising from men's mutual need of one another, attention will be concentrated on their relationships and the answer to the prior question—'What is justice?'—will be more easily discovered;

[99]

for justice is essentially a matter of human relationships. Hence Plato, when asked the primary reason for life in communities, puts forward, not—like his more positivist predecessors—the simple premise of man's weakness in the face of the other animals, but the multiplicity and variety of his needs. As has recently been pointed out,[9] the earlier view (surviving later in Polybius and Lucretius) emphasized man's resemblance to the beasts. Like the other beasts they lived, and what brought them together was their comparative helplessness. The mightier animals prowl alone, relying on their individual strength and fierceness, but the weaker pool their strength by going about in herds. In the *Republic*, on the other hand, what brings men together is a purely human faculty that distinguishes them from the beasts, namely diversity of function. 'Must we not say', Socrates continues, 'that one man will be a farmer, another a builder, and another a weaver or a shoemaker?' A city is necessary in order that there may be division of labour. Hence unlike a herd of animals, it is an organic whole, with parts having different functions.

Aristotle's interest, like Plato's, is not in discovering what made men first come together in communities, but what makes them live in communities now. At the beginning of the *Politics* he states his method frankly. He wishes to demonstrate, he says, that the statesman in a true state (by which he means of course the Greek city-state, the *polis*) is generically different from a king, the head of a household, or the master of slaves. It is not simply a question of numbers, but a totally different relationship. To make this clear he will proceed by his favourite method of analysing a complex structure into its simple elements, and where the object of examination is a living and growing organism, the best way to carry this out is to consider it as if in the process of evolution from a simpler to a more complex state. There follows his famous remark that whereas a city originally comes into being for the sake of mere life, it *exists* for the sake of the good life. The crux of the problem is not to lay bare the origin of communal life, which doubtless lies in the attempt to satisfy man's basic material needs: that is only a means towards the philosopher's real aim, which is to discover how the contemporary state may best fulfil its purpose of enabling each and all of its members to live the best life possible with due regard to the rights of the others.

Both Plato and Aristotle see the state as existing first and foremost for the sake of what they call self-sufficiency (in Greek *autarkeia*, whence we now speak of autarky). An individual is not self-sufficient by himself, but a political community is—or at least should be: in so far as it is not, it is imperfect. This means of course in the first place that it must be what is nowadays called 'viable'. But it means more than that. According to Aristotle, the best kind of state is not only a self-sufficient entity as a whole; it is also a community so organized as to give the greatest possible measure of autarky to every individual citizen. Nor did he confine the meaning of autarky to the bare satisfaction of economic needs. In the *Ethics* he defines it as 'that which by itself makes life desirable, and lacking in nothing', and he goes on to identify it with happiness, the final end of all human activity. We need no reminding today that the satisfaction of a man's economic needs is no guarantee that he will find life 'desirable and lacking in nothing' and be perfectly happy. Hence Aristotle's insistence that a political system is not complete until it has provided not only for life but for the good life. Only in society, he claimed, could this be attained by man. Everyone should aim at autarky, 'but', he goes on, 'I do not mean that he should be self-sufficient to himself alone, but with parents, children and wife, friends and fellow-citizens, for man is by nature fitted for political society'. Happiness, in Aristotle's belief, consists in fulfilling one's own proper nature, and the thing which above all others characterizes a human being and raises him above the beasts is his capacity for community life: he is 'by nature a political creature'. This is argued from the fact that over and above the faculties which he shares with the other animals, he alone possesses *logos*, the power of ordered thought. All animals feel pleasure and pain, but through the exercise of *logos* man can pass beyond these immediate sensations to an awareness of what is beneficial or harmful, good or evil, just or unjust. This discrimination between good and evil is a prerequisite of organized life in communities. Hence the *polis* is a natural human institution, and as he roundly declares, anyone who is unfit to share in its life or too self-sufficient to need it is either a beast or a god.[10]

In many of its details, the subject of this exposition—Greek beliefs about the origins of life and of human communities—has no more than a historical interest. I hope I have succeeded in my primary aim of showing that this interest is in itself considerable. Nevertheless it was right that we should be led on to a glimpse of the philosophical implications of these views, for it is there if anywhere that we may hope to find something with a value unaffected by the passage of time. I should like to end by showing briefly how Greek opinions on these topics, philosophically considered, fall into two broad classes reflecting two fundamentally opposed views of the world and of human nature. This may have the additional advantage of revealing the essential unity of our subject. To us the origin of the universe, the origin of life, and the beginnings of human society seem to belong to quite different branches of science. This departmentalism has been a necessity of scientific progress, but human thought has not made the advance without some sacrifice of coherence. As compensation for their comparative ignorance, the Greeks were able to take a more synoptic view, and it so happened that they produced men of a genius supremely fitted to do so. We may still look to them for examples of the kind of conceptual framework that will always be needed if life is to be more than a series of *ad hoc* decisions with no guiding idea behind them.

In speaking of the origin of life, I diverged as little as possible into the large subject of Greek cosmogony, but it became apparent that the two could not be separated. They were parts of the same process and governed by the same laws. We saw for instance how for Anaximander the cosmos first arose from the separation of hot and cold and their subsequent action in producing wet and dry. Life was a continuation of the same process, resulting from the further action of heat on moisture. It follows that, for the Greek, whatever principles underlie the creation of the world will also govern the origin of life. Now the earliest philosophical cosmogonies were purely naturalistic in their assumptions. The conception of a creating god was foreign to them, as it was in general even to Greek religion. Zeus and his fellow-gods might rule the world, but they did not create it. So for the philosophers there was no transcendent rational being, separate from the world and creating it either out of nothing or by the organization of a pre-existing chaos of matter. It was assumed that the raw material of the world was in everlasting motion, and the rest followed, as some of them put it, 'by necessity'. In the semi-articulate thought of the early Milesians this may have involved a kind of pantheism, but no more. Anaxagoras indeed, impressed by criticisms of this vagueness, introduced a First Cause, gave it the name of Mind, and said that it brought order into the original chaos. For this achievement Aristotle called him the first sober thinker among a set of people who talked at random, but found to his disappoint-ment that Anaxagoras only used his new idea as a device to start off the motion. Then Mind withdrew, and his world was governed not on any theistic lines but in a way as materialistic and mecha-nical as those of his predecessors. This we saw in an earlier chapter. In the peculiar system of Empedocles we found the world of nature similarly abandoned to the chance interplay of material forces, and the culmination of this view was reached in the atomic theory of Leucippus and Democritus. They called the first cause necessity or nature, but in the view of Plato and Aristotle one might as well call it chance, for it is a purely blind and irrational force. Man like the rest of nature is only something thrown up by the random collisions of particles in aimless flight, and his mind a material conglomeration of swiftly moving atoms.

That is one view of nature. The other is the view which Plato, following the lead of Socrates, evolved in opposition. Their con-tention was that nature shows itself to be the work of reason, and that therefore reason, in the form of a supreme Being transcending nature, is a cause prior to and overruling chance or the necessary clash of opposing physical forces. The change is connected with a change of motive. The positivism of the Ionians was a product of scientific curiosity, whereas Socrates and Plato were intensely con-cerned with moral issues. This does not of course carry any impli-cation for the truth of their results. Aristotle inherited from them the explanation of the processes of nature as directed towards a rational purpose and the supposition of a supreme intelligence as their First Cause; yet the cause of scientific thought in Greece certainly owed no less to him than to the earlier Ionians. The fact however must be recognized that in opposing the Ionian world-view Socrates and Plato were especially concerned with what they considered its disastrous effects on morality.

When natural philosophy was first launched in the 6th century, it had little effect in the field of human conduct. Thales and Anaximander might be statesmen as well as philosophers, but ethical and political teaching was still left to the legislator or the poet as such: they were not subjects for philosophy, and no rationally based ethical systems were evolved. But in the middle of the 5th century, especially at Athens, a change occurred which was due at least in part to the establishment of extreme democratic forms of government. Education for citizenship became an urgent need, and the gap was filled by the class of free-lance lecturers known as Sophists, who travelled from city to city earning their living by their instruction. Being for the most part brilliant and persuasive speakers, they gained a great following among the young and ambitious. Older and more conservative citizens disliked them for the sceptical trend of their views and their contempt for religion and tradition in general. In this milieu a nascent philosophy of human conduct was marked by an absence of religious scruple and of any universal moral principles. It was some of the Sophists who seized on the mechanistic Ionian theories of the origin of all things in support of their view that moral standards have no basis in nature but are purely relative and temporary. How this happened we may best see by looking at it through the eyes of Plato.

In his later years Plato planned to expound and justify his whole conception of human life in a magnificent new series of dialogues which he abandoned in mid-course. The first of these, and the only one to be completed, is the *Timaeus*, and the way that he begins it is this. In his earlier work the *Republic* he had made Socrates describe the ideal state. We are now to imagine a group of friends assembled just after the narration of this or a similar scheme. Socrates reopens the discussion by explaining that not being a practical statesman, he only feels at home in the field of abstract thought. He has done his part, and now wants his friends, who are men with more experience of practical affairs, to give their impressions of how his state would work in the real world, where it would not exist alone but would come into contact, and doubtless into conflict, with other powers. Critias replies that they were prepared for this, and have a plan. He knows a legend of the Athens of long ago, which by a remarkable coincidence was governed on much the same lines as the city of Socrates's dream, and how it met and defeated the aggressive and imperialistic power of Atlantis which had invaded the Mediterranean from a large island in the Atlantic ocean. (Some have seen in Atlantis an early vision of America.) This story should serve our purpose, he says. We will pretend that your imaginary citizens were our actual ancestors, and thus transfer your scheme from the plane of theory to that of real life.

This plan seems admirably suited to ensure complete fulfilment of Socrates's request, and we look forward to the story. But a surprise awaits us. Instead of continuing it immediately, Critias goes on: 'Timaeus is to speak first, because he is the best astronomer and natural scientist among us and can tell us how the world began and what is the origin and nature of the human race.' The rest of the first dialogue is entirely taken up with a long, and in places highly technical and difficult discourse of Timaeus involving us in cosmogony, astronomy, mathematics, anthropogony and physiology.

Horace says that if we want to tell the tale of the Trojan War we should not go back to the egg from which Helen was born. Why should Plato think it right to begin an epic on the glories of ancient Athens by going even further back, to the beginning of the world itself? Owing partly to its intrinsic interest, and partly to the fact that most of what was to follow in the other dialogues was apparently never written, attention has always been centred on the cosmology and astronomy of the *Timaeus*. But for Plato the importance of this was undoubtedly that it led up to a particular view of the nature of man. His real purpose can hardly be better expressed than in the words of a great American Platonic scholar. Paul Shorey wrote that the *Timaeus*

> remains essentially a prose-poem of the Universe, Plato's *De rerum natura*, conceived in the poetic spirit of the Presocratic philosophers, but from the point of view of an ultimate philosophy diametrically opposed to theirs. It is Plato's endeavour to combine with all possible concessions to the mechanistic philosophies, of which the atomism of Democritus was the latest and most conspicuous expression, a fundamental faith in a spiritual origin of and a benign purpose in the ordered Universe that we know.[11]

For reasons which we can only conjecture, the great design of which the *Timaeus* formed the beginning was never carried to completion. But in the tenth book of the *Laws*, his last work, Plato explains concisely but adequately why it was necessary for a philosophy of human life to begin by meeting the cosmogonists on their own ground and put forward a rival view of the origin of the Universe and man. Young men of today, he begins, get infected with wrong beliefs about the gods, including actual atheism, and make them an excuse for evil living. They can be compelled by punishment to conform to the laws, but if we can persuade them by an appeal to reason, so much the better. In doing so, the most troublesome argument that we have to face is the one put forward by the Sophists, which contrasts 'nature' with 'convention' (or law, or art). This argument depends on accepting the assumption of Ionian cosmogony that nature is a blind, irrational force. The Universe and all that it contains—plants, animals and men, and the wheeling heavenly bodies on whose movements depend the regularity of day and night, summer and winter—are products of nature. They are prior to reason, which only came to birth with man, and are therefore the result of purely fortuitous combinations. Later came art or design, a more insignificant force of purely human origin, and created some shadows with little reality about them. Now law and its assumptions are products of art and reason, not nature, and justice is only a creation of law. Hence the 'life according to nature', which this creed exalts, consists in satisfying one's personal desires uninhibited by any subservience to law or convention.

Against this Plato sets the view that far from there being any contrast between nature and the world of law and order, nature and law are the same thing. Reason and order are not merely human characteristics, for the nature of the universe is such that it can only have been the product of a reason existing antecedently to make it. But if the origin of the Universe can be revealed as the unfolding of an ordered plan, then to make any distinction between life according to nature and life according to law, and try to exalt either at the expense of the other, is to talk nonsense. Law, order and art are the products of intelligence and intelligence is the first and highest manifestation of nature. Such a metaphysic, if it can be proved, will have an obvious bearing on the significance of human life.

We can now see better what Plato is aiming at in the cosmogony of the *Timaeus*. He was summoning all the resources of contemporary science to prove that the major events of the cosmos could only be explained on the assumption that behind them lay a conscious and designing Mind, in other words that they were a divine creation. If in this he was in conflict with the Ionians, he had on his side the mathematical and astronomical studies of the Pythagoreans, whose whole outlook was more sympathetic to his own. Both he and they went further. Not only was the Universe created by a god, it was itself a living creature, and the sun, moon and stars the highest forms of life within it. The divinity of the heavenly bodies was of course a traditional article of Greek belief, and it had been a truly shocking thing when the Ionian scientist Anaxagoras announced that the sun was only an incandescent lump of rock.

There is a contrast here between the Greek way of thinking and our own. We tend to associate life and reason with freedom of action. Instead of following a regular and to all appearances predestined track, the living creature will exhibit a multiplicity of movements and activities. When we see something everlastingly revolving in a circle, we do not jump to the conclusion that it is a living and divine being. For Plato on the other hand there was a perfect analogy between rational thought and circular motion. If like him we wanted to argue that the planets, as well as the fixed stars, were alive and divine, we might think it evidence in favour of our view that they do not appear to travel monotonously in circles, but can be seen to deviate, go back on their tracks, and even stand still. Yet to Plato this was the scandal that had to be removed. In order to show that their movements were inspired by reason, he had to explain away their irregularities and demonstrate that, contrary to appearances, they were really moving all the time in perfect circles.[12]

In this world-view of Plato's, the blindly mechanistic force of 'necessity', which governed the Ionian cosmogonies, is not abolished altogether. It persists, but is almost entirely subordinated by the mind of the divine creator. Almost, but not quite. Plato is not a monist, nor is his god omnipotent. He has to work on a pre-existing material with certain given characteristics, and although in general he impresses it with the stamp of his own reason and goodness, there remains an irreducible minimum of resistance which accounts for the disorder and evil in the world. As for man, his possession of reason relates him to God and gives him infinite possibilities, but being associated with a material body he is subject also to the 'necessity' of physical forces and finds it difficult to realize his potentialities completely.

The Greeks drew the analogy between microcosm and macrocosm, man and the Universe, with a seriousness and a literalness which we have outgrown. Plato followed the Pythagoreans in holding that the pre-eminent characteristic of the world was its ordered beauty (that is the meaning of the Greek word *cosmos*), and that the soul of man, being rational, was capable of becoming a *cosmos* in miniature. The order and regularity in the world were evidence of its divine origin, an origin in which human beings shared. Hence the true end of man, as Plato puts it elsewhere, was to 'assimilate himself to God'.

To sum up, his aim in the *Timaeus* was to make use of the regularities of the heavenly bodies, and their effects in the cosmos as a whole, in order to demonstrate that the whole Universe works in accordance with a rational and moral law. By showing forth the same rational and moral law in terms of human life, men will not be acting contrary to nature as the Sophists thought; they will be fulfilling their own being as parts of nature, and in this true self-fulfilment is to be found the greatest happiness both for individuals and communities.

There we have the two opposing views. Each has left us a legacy of speculation, the detail of which it is fascinating to trace. From the Ionian tradition we have the conflict of opposites, in which as Milton put it (for it has had its appeal to our English poets),

> Hot, cold, wet and dry, four champions fierce,
> Strive here for mastery.

Spenser repeats that in the beginning

> The earth the air the water and the fire
> Then gan to range themselves in huge array,
> And with contrary forces to conspire
> Each against other by all means they may.[13]

The same tradition tells how in the course of this conflict of natural forces there appeared on the still plastic surface of the earth those strange bubbles or membranes from which emerged the earliest forms of life. In Plato on the other hand we may read the results of early astronomical and mathematical studies, and see how in his mind the cosmic motions of sun and stars were linked to psychological theories about circular movements in the soul of the world, and their reproduction in the minds of men. All this remains of the greatest interest for the historian of thought, and particularly the historian of science. But behind all the detail lies the perennial clash of philosophies, the two irreconcilable answers to a question that is as pertinent to our life as it was to that of ancient Greece: Is nature the product of mind, or is mind only one among the many products of nature?

Today in our Western world the conviction lives on that there is a purpose in history, that nature is not self-subsistent but owes its being to a transcendent First Cause whose mind is reflected, however feebly, in the thoughts and wills of men—in other words that men are sons of the God who created the world. It is the conviction of the Christian religion. On the other side are ranged not only the materialistic determinism of the Marxist but a variety of philosophies of a positivist or humanist tendency. To choose between the fundamental alternatives carries one beyond the findings of science and the niceties of logic. For most of us the decision is made at a deeper level of the human psyche, and that is why it is so difficult for one side to persuade the other by an appeal to facts or argument. Men of equal intelligence, education and honesty may hold to either conviction with a sense that they 'can no other'. Where this is so, what matters is that each should recognize the sincerity of his fellow and practise the virtue of tolerance, and this becomes easier when we know that it is not merely a conflict of our time but one which has divided the human mind in every civilized age. Perhaps then it has been worth while to demonstrate once again that here as in so many other spheres of thought we may echo the words of Lucretius: 'Primum Graius homo'—the Greeks have been before us.

Notes

I. MOTHER EARTH: THE MYTHS

1. Hero, *Pneumatica*, 2.11, pp. 228–32 Schmidt.

2. The stars animate for Aristotle: cf. esp. *De caelo*, 292a19: ἀλλ' ἡμεῖς ὡς περὶ σωμάτων αὐτῶν μόνον καὶ μονάδων τάξιν μὲν ἐχόντων ἀψύχων δὲ πάμπαν, διανοούμεθα· δεῖ δὲ ὡς μετεχόντων ὑπολαμβάνειν πράξεως καὶ ζωῆς. Nature makes nothing in vain, *De caelo*, 291b13 *et al.*

3. Sir Henry Cohen in *Philosophy*, 1952, p. 157. *Cf.* F. G. Crookshank in Ogden and Richards, *Meaning of Meaning* (1930), Suppl. II.

4. H. Butterfield, *History and Human Relations* (London, 1951), p. 66.

5. See *e.g.* W. P. D. Wightman, *Growth of Scientific Ideas* (Edinburgh, 1950), p. 10. Sir Charles Sherrington called water the 'great menstruum of life', which makes life possible. (*Man on his Nature*, Cambridge, 1940, etc., p. 121, Pelican ed., 1955, p. 113.)

6. For Egypt and Babylon, see *Before Philosophy* (ed. Frankfort, Pelican Books, 1949), pp. 54, 84. The remark about Thales and the Hebrews is from A. T. Olmstead's *History of Persia* (Chicago, 1948), p. 211. Okeanos and Tethys in Homer, *Il.* 14. 201, 246. Dr Needham (*Science and Civilisation in China*, Cambridge, 1956, p. 42) quotes a remarkable parallel from a Taoist work of perhaps the 5th century B.C. It gives reasons why water must be considered the raw material of all things, and includes the analogy with animal life.

7. Diog. Laert., *prooem.* 3: ἐξ ἑνὸς τὰ πάντα γίνεσθαι καὶ εἰς ταυτὸν πάλιν ἀναλύεσθαι (referred to Musaeus. For Orpheus, *cf.* Gruppe's arguments sum-

marized in Guthrie, *Orpheus and Greek Religion*, London, 1935 and 1952, 74 f.). The most striking description, in mythical form, of the original unity of heaven and earth is Euripides fr. 484 ὡς οὐρανός τε γαῖα τ' ἦν μορφὴ μία,

ἐπεὶ δ' ἐχωρίσθησαν ἀλλήλων δίχα
τίκτουσι πάντα κτλ.

But it is reflected earlier in Hesiod's story of the violent separation by Kronos of his parents Ouranos and Gaia (*Theog.* 154 ff.). Among other passages may be mentioned Ap. Rhod. 1. 496–8, Diod. 1.7.1 κατὰ γὰρ τὴν ἐξ ἀρχῆς τῶν ὅλων σύστασιν μίαν ἔχειν ἰδέαν οὐρανόν τε καὶ γῆν, μεμιγμένης αὐτῶν τῆς φύσεως. μετὰ δὲ ταῦτα διαστάντων τῶν σωμάτων ἀπ' ἀλλήλων, τὸν μὲν κόσμον περιλαβεῖν ἅπασαν τὴν ὁρωμένην ἐν αὐτῷ σύνταξιν.

8. *Man on his Nature*, Cambridge ed., p. 266, Pelican 219.

9. Earth invoked in oath-taking, Homer, *Il.* 19. 529, cf. 3.104; γῆ πάντων μητήρ Hes. *Erga* 563, etc. I am not of course suggesting that this belief was peculiar to the Greeks, but a comparative study can hardly be attempted within the limits of these pages. One example may however be quoted to indicate the wide range of similar ideas. M. Gluckman, in *Custom and Conflict in Africa* (Blackwell, Oxford, 1955), writes that for the Nuer and many African societies 'the earth has a mystical as well as a secular value. . . . The earth . . . comes to symbolize . . . the general prosperity, fertility and good fortune. . . . In West Africa men worship the earth. . . . In Central and South Africa kings, who symbolize the political unity of tribes, are identified with the earth; the Barotse word for king means "earth" ' (pp. 16 f.). Etymology suggests remarkable parallels in the early Greek mind between parts of the earth and the anatomy of a woman. See the notes of C. C. van Essen in *Venus Cloacina*, *Mnemos.* 1956, 137–44.

10. Eur. *Phoen.*, 638 ff., Ovid, *Met.*, 3.106 ff.

11. For the names of the survivors, see schol. Eur. *Phoen.*, 942 (possibly from Aeschylus, but *cf.* Nauck on Aesch. fr. 376, T.G.F., p. 111), Pherekydes fr. 22 (a) Jacoby, Hellanicus fr. 1 (a) Jacoby. For the Thebans as descendants of the Spartoi, see esp. Eur. H.F. 5 (and *cf.* 793 ff., *Phoen.*, 939–42):

Θήβας . . . ἔνθ' ὁ γηγενὴς
σπαρτῶν στάχυς ἔβλαστεν, ὧν γένους Ἄρης
ἔσωσ' ἀριθμὸν ὀλίγον, οἳ Κάδμου πόλιν
τεκνοῦσι παίδων παισί.

For the title given to the Thebans themselves, Pind. *Isthm.* 1.30, 7.10, fr. 9 Bowra; Eur. *Suppl.* 578, Soph. O.C. 1533; to Echion, Eur. *Bacch.* 1274. But note that it is applied to the human race in general by Athena in Aesch. *Eum.* 410. This may be an example of the analogy between human and agricultural fertilization which we shall touch on later, and which was constantly present to the Greek mind (*cf.* the quotation from the *Menexenus* on p. 25, and Soph. *Tr.* 31–3); or perhaps, like Plato *Soph.* 247c, where it is used of those whom Plato is characterizing as giants, it only shows that the word became a general equivalent of γηγενής.

12. Eur. H.F. 5, *Phoen.* 935. At *Bacch.* 538 Pentheus, as son of Echion, is described as χθόνιον γένος ἐκφύς τε δράκοντος, and also compared to a giant. At 996 he is γηγενής. Of the sown men in the Jason story, Ap. Rhod. 3.1346 (γηγενέων ἀνδρῶν), 1355. Earth is their mother, *ib.* 1374 f. The chthonian character of serpents was so generally recognized that to say of men that they were born from a serpent's teeth is only another way of saying that they were born from the earth.

13. Birth of the giants, Hes. *Theog.* 185. Some examples of the giants as γηγενεῖς: *Batrachomyiomachia* 7: γηγενέων ἀνδρῶν μιμούμενοι ἔργα γιγάντων; Soph. *Tr.* 1058 ὁ γηγενής στρατὸς γιγάντων; of Typhon, Aesch. *Pr.* 351. In Aristoph. *Frogs* 825 γηγενεῖ φυσήματι almost suggests the modern sense of the words 'a gigantic puff'. Besides the wording of *Batr.* 7, there is plenty of evidence to suggest that the giants not only resembled men in being γηγενεῖς, but were in fact thought of as an earlier human generation. See Preller, *Philol.* 1852, 39 f., and *cf.* also Diod. 1.26.7, Teleclides *Amphictyones* fr. 1.15 Kock (in a facetious description of the men of the Golden Age): οἱ δ᾽ ἄνθρωποι πίονες ἦσαν τότε καὶ μέγα χρῆμα γιγάντων.

14. Pelasgos: Paus. 8.1.4, Hes. *ap.* Apollod. 2.1.1. Palaichthon: Aesch. *Suppl.* 250. Erechtheus: *Il.* 2.548 ff., Hdt. 8.55, Eur. *Ion* 281–2. Erichthonios: Eur. *Ion* 20–21 (γηγενής, *cf.* 267–8), and for later reff. Apollod. 3.14.6 and Frazer *ad loc.* For the daughters of Cecrops, Eur. *Ion ib.* (comparing vv. 1427–9) and later authorities. The names of two of them mean 'dew' or 'dewy'. Cecrops as serpent, Eur. *Ion.* 1163 f., Ar. *Wasps* 438.

Phoroneus of Argos is an interesting figure, for he became recognized as the common ancestor of the oldest Greek people and an antediluvian (he lived before the flood of Deucalion, Plato *Tim.* 22a), but is not directly referred to as αὐτόχθων or γηγενής. He was however the son not of a man but of a river (Inachos), and his mother was Melia, the ash tree—obvious pointers in the same direction (Paus. 2.15.5, Apollod. 2.1.1).

H   [113]

15. The Carians autochthonous, Hdt. 1.171; the Arcadians, Xen. *Hell.* 7.1.23; the Phaeacians, Ap. Rhod. 4.548 (in Homer they are descended from the king of the giants, *Od.* 7.56); the Athenians, Eur. *Ion* 589 f., Ar. *Wasps* 1076 ('Αττικοὶ μόνοι δικαίως ἐγγενεῖς αὐτόχθονες), Plato *Menex.* 237d, Isocr. *Paneg.* 24, *cf. Panath.* 124. Pericles puts it in terms more suitable to the enlightenment of the 5th century (Thuc. 2.36): τὴν γὰρ χώραν ἀεὶ οἱ αὐτοὶ οἰκοῦντες. χθόνιος is used in the same sense, Soph. *Aj.* 202: χθονίων ἀπ' Ἐρεχθειδᾶν. The Arcadian claim was one which the Athenians had to admit beside their own, Dem. *Fals. Leg.* 261: μόνοι γὰρ πάντων αὐτόχθονες ὑμεῖς ἐστὲ κἀκεῖνοι.

16. Thuc. 1.6: 'It is not long since the older Athenian citizens ceased to wear linen tunics and make a topknot of their hair with golden cicadas twisted in it.' In Ar. *Knights* (1331), to be τεττιγοφόρας is to be ἀρχαίῳ σχήματι λαμπρός, and at *Clouds* 984 τεττίγων ἀνάμεστα is the equivalent of ἀρχαῖα. For explicit explanation of the custom, we have to go to the scholars of later times, but we shall not now doubt Eustathius (of Byzantium, 12th cent. A.D.) when he says that golden cicadas were worn εἰς σύμβολον τοῦ γηγενεῖς εἶναι (Eust. 395.34: vol. i, Leipzig 1827, p. 320, line 1).

The Greeks had some strange and interesting beliefs about the cicada. Plato (*Phaedrus* 259 b) relates a story that they were once men, who were so intoxicated by the discovery of song that they neglected food and drink and so died. They were turned into cicadas, to whom the Muses have granted the gift of a whole life of song without need of either food or drink. Alternatively they were supposed to live only on dew, as in the pleasant Anacreontic trifle which begins:

> Happy call we thee, cicada,
> Seated there among the tree-tops
> With a drop of dew to stay thee,
> Singing like a king in glory.

(Later in the same poem the cicada is addressed as γηγενής). Since in fact the cicada's only nourishment, during its two or three months of arboreal life, is the sap of the twigs on which it perches, the misunderstanding may be forgiven.

As to their mode of generation, the comic anthropogony with which Aristophanes regales the guests at Plato's symposium says that at one time mankind 'sowed their seed not in one another, but in the ground, like cicadas' (*Symp.* 191c: ἐγέννων καὶ ἔτικτον οὐκ εἰς ἀλλήλους ἀλλ' εἰς γῆν, ὥσπερ οἱ τέττιγες). Perhaps one should not take the comic poet's farrago too seriously, but there are many elements of genuine folklore in it, and this looks like a reminiscence of belief in a stage intermediate between completely spontaneous generation from the earth and purely sexual generation, a stage at which the cicada's evolution has stopped, though our own has left it behind. The earth is still the mother, but her children impregnate her with their seed, as of course the plants may also be said to do. One may compare other myths in which the earth, though still in a literal sense the mother of living creatures, needs fertilization by a male element: e.g. the birth of Erichthonios from the earth when the seed of Hephaestus had fallen on it. (See H. J. Rose, *Handbook of Greek Mythol.*, 1928, 110.)

Plutarch (*Amat.* 767 c) mentions a variant according to which male cicadas are said to deposit the sperm in the plants of the squill. Aristotle's account (H.A. 556a25 ff.) makes it quite clear that he knows the generation of cicadas to be the result of normal sexual union, and he describes their mode of copulation. He does however go on to say that the females lay their eggs sometimes on fallow land, sometimes in the canes (κάλαμοι) on which vines are supported, and also in the stems of squills. It looks as if the idea that the males deposit the sperm in the earth or in squills is a popular confusion of the two stages of impregnation and egg-laying.

17. The story of Deucalion and the flood is not told in full in any extant writer before Ovid (*Met.* 1.262 ff.); but Pindar (*Ol.* 9.42) speaks of Deucalion and Pyrrha descending from Parnassus and founding 'a progeny of stone', and references to the story also occur in Plato (*Critias* 112a, *Tim.* 22a) and Aristotle (*Meteor.* 352a32). Cf. also Hesiod fr. 135, quoted below, n. 20. Landing-places: Parnassus, Pindar *l.c.*, Ov. *Met.* 1.316; Othrys, Hellanicus fr. 117 Jacoby; Athos, Serv. Verg. *Ecl.* 6.41; Aetna, Hygin. *Fab.* 153. Apollonius Rhodius mentions Deucalion as a first king and founder of culture. Deucalion's was not the only flood-story in Greece. The flood in the time of Ogygos, the autochthonous (Paus. 9.5.1) ancestor of the Thebans, was said to be older than Deucalion's, and was localized in Boeotia. (See Roscher, *Lex. der Myth.* 3.684.)

18. Plato, *Menexenus* 237d–238a. The claim to have provided all mankind with bread was based on Athenian control of the Eleusinian mysteries celebrated in honour of Demeter (goddess of the earth or of grain, see Guthrie, *Gks. and their Gods*, 1950, 283, n. 2) and her daughter Kore. Isocrates makes the connexion clear in the *Panegyricus* (28), where he tells the Eleusinian story of how Demeter came to Attica in her search for Kore who had been carried off by Pluto. In gratitude to 'our ancestors' for services which may only be told to the initiates, she granted them a double gift: her fruits,

and the mystic ritual which ensures a blessed future life for those who partake of it. In the *Menexenus* the fruits are specified as wheat and barley.

19. For the Egyptians as the oldest race, see Aristotle, *Meteor.* 352b21. In spite of the story in Hdt. 2.2, it is unlikely that their claim to be the fathers of human kind was ever abandoned (cf. Diod. 1.10.1). The Greeks believed that the combination of Nile water with the peculiar composition (εὐκρασία) of the Egyptian soil constituted ideal conditions for the production of life. It was even thought that the earth in that region had retained its pristine capacity to produce animal life by spontaneous generation, which elsewhere (at least as regards the larger creatures) it had lost. So Diod. 1.10. 2–3, and the passages quoted in Diels-Kranz, vol. 2, pp. 136–7; also Ovid, *Met.* 1.422 ff. (All these statements probably go back to Democritus or even earlier, see Ch. 2, n. 10, below.) According to J. A. Wilson in *Before Philosophy* (Pelican, 1949), Egyptian peasants still believe in the life-giving power of the mud left behind by the retreating Nile. Aesch. *Suppl.* 454 ff.

μήποτε πάλιν ἴδοις
ἀλφεσίβοιον ὕδωρ,
ἔνθεν ἀεξόμενον
ζώφυτον αἷμα βροτοῖσι θάλλει

has also been taken to refer to this belief, and no doubt rightly, though in isolation it might imply no more than abundant fertility.

20. Ov. *Met.* 381 ff. In a fragment of Hesiod (115 Rzach) it is actually said that Zeus granted to Deucalion 'people from the earth': λεκτοὺς ἐκ γαίης λαοὺς πόρε Δευκαλίωνι. The pun λαός – λᾶας did not of course escape the Greeks (Apollod. 1.7.2, and probably also conscious in Pind. *Ol.* 9.45–6), and may have helped to give this particular story of earth-born men its own twist.

21. Prometheus as culture-hero, fire-bringer, etc., but not creator of mankind, Aesch. P.V. 109 ff., 442 ff., Hes. *Th.* 565, *Erga* 50 ff. Men are contemptuously described as πλάσματα πηλοῦ by the birds in Aristoph. *Birds* 687: cf. Aesch. fr. 369 N. (of Pandora) τοῦ πρωτοπλάστου σπέρματος θνητὴ γυνή. The earliest surviving mentions of Prometheus in this connexion occur in the 4th century, in a fragment of Heraclides Ponticus (66 Wehrli) and Philemon fr. 89 Kock

τί ποτε Προμηθεύς, ὃν λέγουσ' ἡμᾶς πλάσαι
καὶ τἄλλα πάντα ζῷα;

Menander fr. 535 (in Lucian *Erotes* 43) says in a conventional diatribe against women that Prometheus was rightly punished because he γυναῖκας ἔπλασεν, which may perhaps be a reference to the story of Pandora the first woman, since it does not sound as if it were intended to include men. (A tradition appearing only in late sources substitutes Prometheus for the Hephaestus of Hesiod as the artificer of Pandora. See Plotinus, *Enn.* 4.13.4. It is not unnatural that the bringer of fire and the god of fire himself should be confused.) The cleverness of Prometheus in making human beings gives the point to an epigram of Erinna (4 Diehl), if indeed it is genuine. Athenaeus who quotes it says no more than Ἤριννα ἢ ὁ πεποιηκὼς τὸ εἰς αὐτὴν ἀναφερόμενον ποιημάτιον. Preller (*Philol.*, 1952, p. 57) professes to find the story as early as Sappho, from a reference in Servius (on Verg. *Ecl.* 6.42). This is a mistake. The coupling of Sappho's name with Hesiod's makes it clear, if it did not already emerge from the general run of the sentence, that Servius is attributing no more to her than the anger of the gods at the theft of fire, and its consequences. We may note also that the lemma in Virgil contains no more than 'Caucasiasque refert volucres et furta Promethei'. The comment of Servius runs in full (ed. Thilo 72):

> Caucasiasque refert v.f.p. et hic fabulae ordinem vertit, quae talis est; Prometheus, Iapeti et Clymenes filius, post factos a se homines dicitur auxilio Minervae caelum ascendisse et adhibita facula ad rotam solis ignem furatus, quem hominibus indicavit. ob quam causam irati dii duo mala immiserunt terris, mulieres et morbos, sicut Sappho et Hesiodus memorant.

F. Wehrli (*Hesiods Prometheus*, in *Navicula Chiloniensis: stud. philol. F. Jacoby ... oblata*, 1956, 35 f.) suggests reasons for supposing that the omission of any early reference to Prometheus as the creator of woman may be accidental, and that he was so regarded even before Hesiod. But this must remain conjecture. References in later literature are of course common. See Preller-Robert, *Gr. Myth.* 1.1.81, n. 6 or Frazer's Apollodorus (Loeb ed.), i. 51, n. 5. For Prometheus in general we now have the articles of W. Kraus and L. Eckhart in RE xxiii, 1 (45th half-volume), 1957, cols. 653–730.

The Pandora story (*cf.* Aesch. fr. 369 above) is a fascinating byroad in this mythological network—she was the first woman, and made of earth and water (Hes. *Erga* 61)—which nevertheless we can hardly allow ourselves to follow up here. Her name makes it pretty clear that, as later authorities say explicitly, she was originally a personification of the earth itself. (Hesych. *s.v.* has Πανδώρα ἡ γῆ, also schol. Aristoph. *Birds* 970 quoted by Roscher, *Lex.* 3.1520: see other evidence collected *ib.* 1524 ff.) Hesiod elsewhere called her daughter of Deucalion, but said that she lay with Zeus and bore him Graecus, the ancestor of the earliest Greek people—doubtless originally a marriage of Earth and Heaven (Hes. *ap.* Lydus *De mens.*, p. 8 Rzach).

I have omitted from the text the Orphic story of the origin of man from the soot produced when the Titans, having killed and eaten the child Dionysus, were blasted by the thunderbolt of Zeus. It contains a variant of the 'earth-born' idea, since the Titans from whose remains mankind arose were themselves sons of Earth; but (a) it was not generally current, but confined to a small circle, (b) it is not fully attested before the Christian era, and so has come under suspicion (though not in my opinion rightly) of being a late myth altogether.

22. Lucr. 5. 792-6. Lucretius may be contradicting existing myths. What he denies is suggested by a sentence in the lyric fragment embedded in Hippol., *Ref.* 5.7; Ἀλαλκομενεὺς λίμνας ὑπὲρ Καφισίδος πρῶτος ἀνθρώπων ἄνεσχεν.. (The Boeotian hero Alalkomeneus is called αὐτόχθων by Paus. 9.33.5 and Plut., *Daed. Plat.* 6.) Possibly, but less probably, he had in mind philosophical theories like Anaximander's of the origin of life: ἐν ὑγρῷ γεννηθῆναι τὰ πρῶτα ζῷα A.30. (For this mode of reference see chap. 2, no.3 below.)

II. MOTHER-EARTH: THE SCIENTIFIC APPROACH

1. Lucian, *Philopseudes* 3.

2. Some reflection of this belief no doubt lies behind the curious Homeric curse ἀλλ' ὑμεῖς μὲν πάντες ὕδωρ καὶ γαῖα γένοισθε (*Il.* 7.99. '... be dissolved into your elements'?)

In this connexion one can hardly omit to mention the philosopher-poet Xenophanes (?*c.* 565-460; his exact dates are uncertain), who wrote γῆ καὶ ὕδωρ πάντ' ἐσθ'ὅσα γίνοντ' ἠδὲ φύονται, and again πάντες γὰρ γαίης τε καὶ ὕδατος ἐκγενόμεσθα (B 29 and 33). Whatever else may be said about these statements, we have seen enough to know that they were in no way original. Their relation to another fragment (B 27), in which Xenophanes apparently asserts that earth alone is the basic substance of everything, is difficult to determine, but the genuineness of this latter verse has often been called in question. (It seems to contradict Aristotle's statement that no monist philosopher made earth the ἀρχή, *Metaph.* A 989a5: on this see K. Deichgräber, *Xenophanes* περὶ φύσεως, *Rh. Mus.* 1938, 12 ff.) On the other hand, as Deichgräber has pointed out (*ib.* 14 f.), it is not necessarily in conflict with B 29 and 33. The three lines taken together could mean that whereas Xenophanes thought of earth as the ultimate origin of everything, he regarded earth and water together as the components of living organisms.

Rivers played their part as well as rain. Compare the story of Phoroneus, a 'first man' who was the son of a river (ch. 1, n. 14 above). The few considerable rivers in Greece, such as the Inachus, the Spercheius, the Asopus, and above all the Achelous, were all claimed as ancestral gods or heroes by one or other of the Greek peoples. They were often depicted in the form of bulls (the type of fertility for a Greek). Achelous appeared as a bull, as a snake (chthonian) and in semi-human form (Soph. *Tr.* 11–13). Spercheius is as early as Homer the father of the Myrmidon leader Melanthios, whose mother's name Polydora suggests that she personified the earth (*Il.* 16.174–6). The natural connecting link between the rain-god and rivers is furnished by Homer's epithet διιπετής. Aegina and Thebes were daughters of the Asopus (Hdt. 5.80: other reff. in Roscher's *Lexikon* i.642).

For sacred marriages of Zeus and earth-goddesses see Guthrie, *Gks. and their Gods*, 53 ff., 68 f. Quoted in the text are Aesch. fr. 44 (trans. Cornford, *Princ. Sap.*, 1952, 196) and Eur. fr. 839 (*cf.* fr. 898, a direct imitation of Aeschylus). There is also Pausanias's reference to Γῆς ἄγαλμα ἱκετευούσης ὗσαί οἱ τὸν Δία on the Acropolis at Athens (1.24.3).

3. Anaximander A 10 (St. Hippolytus), A 11 (Ps.-Plutarch, *Strom.*), A 30 (Aëtius, Censorinus, Plutarch). (The letter A followed by a number refers to the extracts given in the relevant section of Diels-Kranz, *Die Fragmente der Vorsokratiker* (5th or later ed.): A = testimonia, B = fragments. This mode of reference will be used from now on for any philosophers included in the collection of Diels and Kranz (DK).)

4. Augustine, *Civ. Dei.* 8.2 (DK A 17). The words referred to in Plutarch (DK A 30) are ὥσπερ οἱ γαλεοί. (mss. παλαιοί: the difference to a Byzantine copyist may have been no more than that between ΓΑΛΕΟΙ and ΠΑΛΕΟΙ.) For the supposed habits of these creatures, *cf.* Plutarch again in *De amore prolis* (494c): 'The *galeoi* in particular reproduce viviparously, and allow their young to issue forth and feed, then take them back and enfold

them in the womb to rest.' The species intended is probably the smooth dog-fish, *mustelus levis* (Aristotle's γαλεὸς ὁ λεῖος), which is the subject of a remarkably detailed and accurate anatomical description by Aristotle (*Hist. anim.* 565b1; see D'Arcy Thomson, *Glossary of Greek Fishes*, 1947, 41). In the same passage Aristotle shows that he shared the common belief about their habits.

5. The remarks in this paragraph must be accepted with all the caution owed to a general impression unsupported by any detailed investigation. Much more work might be done on the relation between scientific dis-coveries and the non-scientific thought of their age. One factor that would have to be taken into account is the intense opposition with which they are often received by contemporaries, and of which Darwinism and psycho-analysis provide particularly striking examples. This is by no means fatal to the thesis, which however I only introduce in reliance on the remark of Aristotle that to raise questions, even without answering them, has its own use and value.

6. Anaxagoras A 11 (Hippolytus), Democritus A 39 (Censorinus and Aëtius).

7. Censorinus *De die natali* 4.9 (Epicurus fr. 333 Usener), Lucr. 5. 805–15 (trans. Bailey), Diod. 1.7.2 (DK vol. ii, p. 135). Epicurean author-ship is in no way excluded by the fact noted by R. Philippson (*Philol. Woch.*, 1929, 672 to 9) that Censorinus was copying Varro, who may be supposed to have used Lucretius. Philippson (*ib.* 672 f.) produces some positive evidence to suggest that the theory of 'terrestrial wombs' originated with Democritus.

I am informed (not having observed it myself) that Diodorus's descrip-tion of what 'may still be observed', i.e. the effect of methane and other marsh gases in producing bubbles which burst with a flash of spontaneous combustion, is by no means a bad one. My informant, who had seen the phenomenon in the bogs of Ireland, characterized it as 'extraordinarily vital'. It is interesting that Aristotle, describing the process of spontaneous genera-tion as he conceived it still to take place in his own time, speaks of a 'frothy bubble' (οἷον ἀφρώδης πομφόλυξ) being formed when muddy liquids are warmed.

8. The other versions referred to are those quoted by DK, vol. ii, pp. 136 f. Males are τὰ ἱκανὴν εἰληφότα πέψιν καὶ θερμότερα. This was also the

belief of Empedocles, though not of Democritus (Arist. *Gen. an.* 764a 6–10). In view of the other evidence here cited, I wonder whether at the end of Empedocles B 67.1 γαίης (which appears in the text of Galen but was altered to γαστήρ by Diels) may not after all be what Empedocles wrote. If Diels's τοκὰς ἄρρενος is retained for the sake of avoiding hiatus, one could translate the line: 'For in the warmer part of the earth appeared that which engendered the male.' Diechgräber suggested γαῖα, which is perhaps easier: 'In its warmer part the earth became mother of the male.' (For these conjectures see crit. n. in DK.) The passage would then refer to the origin of sexual differences at the time when living things first χθονὸς ἐξανέτελλον.

That Empedocles believed the same thing to happen in the womb (Aristotle, *Gen. anim.* 764a1, DK A 81) supports this suggestion, since it was the regular practice to reconstruct the origins of life from analogy with its conditions at the present day.

The word for the bubble-like membranes in Diodorus and the other sources quoted by DK is ὑμήν. There is also an account in the Hippocratic *De carnibus* which uses the word χιτών (8.586 Littré: ? early 4th century B.C.).

Lucretius's comparison between the earth and a woman who is past child-bearing is (5.826 f.):

> sed quia finem aliquem pariendi debet habere
> destitit, ut mulier spatio defessa vetusto.

On the subject of terrestrial milk, the later age of Greece provides a nice example of reconciliation between religion and science. Dio Chrysostom (late 1st century A.D.) in a rhetorical piece (*Or.* 12. 29–30, Loeb ed., vol. ii, p. 32) is enumerating the sources of men's belief in the gods. One is that

> They have abundant nourishment through the generosity and forethought of the god who is their father (i.e. Zeus, as e.g. in Soph. *Aj.* 387). The first of them, those who were born from the earth (αὐτοχθόνες), had the earliest kind of food, that which comes from the earth, for the ooze was then soft and rich and they lapped it from the earth as from a mother, in the same way as plants draw the moisture from it now.

The nourishment is a natural secretion of the earth, but its presence is due to the divine providence. (Note incidentally, in the comparison with plants, yet another example of the analogy from present-day phenomena.) To go later still, the same idea doubtless influenced, even if unconsciously, the choice of a simile in the *Gesta Alexandri* of ps.-Callisthenes, a work of uncertain date but 'apparently the first link in the long chain of romances which constituted

later the *Roman d'Alexandre*'. In this the Brahmin sage Dandamis says to
Alexander's messenger: 'Earth produces all things for me, *as a mother produces
milk for her child*'. (See G. Boas, *Primitivism and Related Ideas in the Middle Ages*,
Baltimore, 1948, pp. 139, 144.)

9. Archelaus A1 and A4. The theory is also taken back into the 5th
century when Plato, recounting Socrates's earlier addiction to natural
philosophy, makes him ask the question: ἆρ' ἐπειδὰν τὸ θερμὸν καὶ τὸ
ψυχρὸν σηπέδονά τινα λαβῇ, τότε δὴ τὰ ζῷα συντρέφεται; (*Phaedo* 96b).
It is explicitly rejected by Aristotle, *Gen. An.* 762b34: it is impossible
ἐπιρρεῖν [*sc.* τὴν τροφήν] ἐκ τῆς γῆς ὥσπερ ἐν τοῖς ἄλλοις ζῴοις ἐκ τῆς
μητρός.

10. DK print the account of Diodorus, and similar extracts from later
writers, as being from the *Mikros Diakosmos* of Democritus. For the justification of this, see their note on p. 136 of vol. ii. On the other hand, if the cosmogony in Diodorus is Democritean, it is strange (to say the least of it) that
it contains no trace of atomism. Its roots are probably older. See E. Bignone,
Empedocle (1916), p. 583, n. 2, J. S. Morrison in *Class. Quart.*, 1941, p. 9,
n. 1, and G. Vlastos, *On the Prehistory in Diodorus*, A.J.P., 1946, pp. 51–9.
The absence of any traces of the atomic world-view was noted by J. H.
Dahlmann, *De philos. Graec. sententiis ad loquellae orig. pertinent.* (Leipzig diss.,
1928); and it seems a little far-fetched to suggest, as Philippson does in
reviewing this work (*Philol. Woch.*, 1929, 670), that these have been carefully
expunged by Hecataeus (Diodorus's supposed source) because he is fiction-
ally reproducing Egyptian philosophy. Diodorus himself, in his introduction
of the account (1.6), clearly has no thought of the Egyptians. (Philippson is
following Reinhardt.)

11. Paraphrased from *Hayy ben Yaqdhân, Roman philosophique d'Ibn Thofail,
text arabe et trad. française*, 2e éd., par L. Gauthier (Beirut, 1936). The relevant
passages are on pp. 18 and 23 ff. of the French translation. Many Greek
heroes were of course suckled in infancy by animals, Telephus actually by a
doe. See H. J. Rose, *Handbook of Greek Mythology* 289.

12. Porphyry, V.P. 44:
    They say that he (Pythagoras) forbade such action (i.e. the eating of
beans) because when the first origin and birth of all things was in confusion, when many things were at the same time being mingled together,
sown together and fermented together in the earth and gradually birth and

separation took place, animals being born and plants springing up all at once, then from the same putrefaction men were formed and beans grew.

Cf. Hippol. *Refutatio* 1.2, Lydus *De mensibus* 99–100 Wuensch.

13. Diod., 1.10.2. *Cf.* Ovid *Met.* 1.422–9, esp. v. 429: Altera pars vivit, rudis est pars altera tellus. On the subject of spontaneous generation see W. Capelle, *Das Problem der Urzeugung bei Arist. u. Theophr. u. in d. Folgezeit* (*Rh. Mus.* 98, 1955, 150–80), to which I owe much material. There is also a selection of passages in Ideler's edition of Arist. *Meteorol.* (1836), vol. ii, 408–10. A full list of creatures believed to be so generated, and the various substances from which they come, is given by Sextus, *Pyrrh. Hypotyp.* 1.41 (Loeb ed., vol. i, 27).

It is interesting that Chinese belief in spontaneous generation included the idea that it 'had once played a *great* part in producing life, and still took place *to a certain extent*' (Needham, *Science and Civilisation in China*, vol. 2, 1956, p. 487, quoting the 12th-cent. A.D. philosopher Chu Hsi. Italics mine). In general, see 'spontaneous generation' in the index to Needham's volume.

14. Insects, *Hist. Anim.* 550b30. For other passages in Aristotle relating to spontaneous generation see Bonitz's index, 124b3 ff. *Gen. An.* 3 ch. 11 is especially important and interesting. The generation of bees he found puzzling. Some believed it to occur spontaneously from flowers (H.A. 553a20), but Aristotle himself inclined to a theory of parthenogenesis. However, at the end of an exhaustive account of alternative possibilities, he sensibly concludes that a final judgement must wait until the facts are more fully known (*Gen. anim.* 3 ch. 10).

For the three modes of generation, see *Metaph.* 1030a12 and a 30. Matter initiates its own changes, *ib.* 1034b4 ὅσων ἡ ὕλη δύναται καὶ ὑφ' αὑτῆς κινεῖσθαι ταύτην τὴν κίνησιν ἣν τὸ σπέρμα κινεῖ. He was of course able to argue that, like all chance or spontaneous events, this happened 'neither always nor for the most part'. (*Cf. Phys.* 2.5. init.) Certain fish produced both from parents and spontaneously, H.A. 569a11.

But there is nothing in Aristotle of the fantastic travellers' tales about mice. In spite of 'the amazing multiplicity and rapidity' of their reproduction (H.A. 580b10), there is no question of its taking place in any but the normal manner. In a very interesting passage of *De generatione animalium* (762b28 ff.), Aristotle argues that 'if there ever were earthborn men or quadrupeds' (a belief on which he does not pronounce either way), it is likely that they originated in the form of worms or grubs. See Platt's note *ad loc.* in the

Oxford trans. Platt calls it 'the only passage from thich we can gather any-thing about A.'s views on evolution'. R. Philippson draws attention to the fact that this theory was attributed to Democritus (who certainly did believe in γηγενεῖς) by Lactantius (A 139, 'D., qui vermiculorum modo putavit effusos esse de terra [sc. homines]'). See *Philol. Woch.*, 1929, 672.

15. In fr. 174 Wimmer, Theophrastus speaks of flies being generated from dung and rotting matter generally. The passage about the frogs follows immediately on this. (This superstition is repeated in all seriousness by St Augustine, *C. Faustum* 6.8.) For spontaneous generation as a secondary cause to generation from seed, see *Caus. Plant.* 1.1.2: 'Thus it is clear that generation from seed is common to all plants; but if some are produced in both ways, spontaneously and from seed, that is not surprising, just as even certain animals are born both from each other and from the earth.' The other passages quoted in the text are C.P. 3.22.3, 4.16.3, *Hist. Plant.* 1.7.1, C.P. 1.6.1. About animals he seems to have moments of scepticism. After describing the spontaneous generation of plants in C.P. 1.5. 1–2, he adds 'as many people account for the generation of animals also'.

Aristotle of course says similar things about heat, drawing attention to the part it plays in incubation (*Gen. an.* 752b29) and in many other ways emphasizing its indispensability to life. He connects it explicitly with spon-taneous generation at *Meteorol.* 379b7 καὶ ζῷα ἐγγίγνεται τοῖς σηπομένοις διὰ τὸ τὴν ἀποκεκριμένην θερμότητα φυσικὴν οὖσαν συνίστασθαι τὰ ἐκκριθέντα. For other relevant passages in Aristotle (θερμότης ψυχική, ζωτική, etc.) see Bonitz's index *s.vv.* θερμός, θερμότης. The function of the *pneuma* is closely connected with it; see *De an.* 420b20, *Part. anim.* 642a13 ff. For heat as the active, and moisture as the passive principle, *cf.* Ar. *Meteorol.* 378b22 τὸ μὲν γὰρ θερμὸν καὶ ψυχρὸν ὡς ποιητικὰ λέγομεν . . . τὸ δὲ ὑγρὸν καὶ ξηρὸν παθητικόν.

Capelle (o.c. n. 13 above) remarks on the fact that, while making much of the sun's heat, Theophrastus knows nothing of the virtue of its light, so essential for the production of chlorophyll in the leaf. This, he says, was only known to the anonymous author (Strato?) of the pseudo-Aristotelian treatise *De coloribus*. The passage that he has in mind must be 795a10–17, which records the observation that those parts of a stem which grow underground, and so are deprived of the sun's light, are white instead of green. The explanation suggested by the author betrays of course no knowledge of any such substance as chlorophyll.

16. For Augustine's belief see Sherrington, *Man on his Nature* (Pelican

ed.), 27. The Pythagorean denial is in Alexander Polyhistor ap. Diog. Laert. 8.28. τὰ ζῷα γεννᾶσθαι ἐξ ἀλλήλων ἀπὸ σπερμάτων, τὴν δ᾽ ἐκ γῆς γένεσιν ἀδύνατον ὑφίστασθαι. The date of the πυθαγορικὰ ὑπομνήματα on which Alexander (1st century B.C.) relied has been much disputed, but they contained much pre-Platonic material. For opinions see, among others, Rohde, *Rh. Mus.* 1872, 47; Zeller, *Phil. d. Gr.*[6] i. 471 with n. 1; M. Wellmann, *Hermes*, 1919, 335–48; Delatte, *Vie de Pyth.* (1922), 198 ff., 232 ff.; Cornford, *Plato and Parmenides* (1939), 3; Festugière, *Rév. Et. Gr.* 1945, 1 ff.; J. E. Raven, *Pyth. and Eleatics* (1948), 159–64.

Capelle (*o.c.*, n. 13 above) quotes a passage from the Hippocratean *De arte* (p. 42. 17 ff. in Gomperz's *Apologie der Heilkunst*, Littré vi. 10.5 ff.) as being 'die einzige grundsätzliche Bekämpfung des Glaubens an Urzeugung in der Antike'. As part of his defence of the power of art, the author is denying the effectiveness of τὸ αὐτόματον in general, but a reader of Capelle might be surprised to learn that the passage contains no reference to spontaneous generation at all. Nor can the οὐ πέδον τίκτει τέκνα of Xuthus in Euripides's *Ion* (542) be said to be parallel to the Pythagorean passage.

For the later history of the belief see Capelle's article, Sherrington, *Man on his Nature* (Pelican ed.) 27, 94 f., and especially C. Singer, *A Short History of Biology* (1931), 433 ff. Here will be found the reference to Redi, and a description of the crucial experiment of Pascal.

17. Lucr. 1. 733.

18. All the evidence for this and the following paragraphs will be found in the section on Empedocles (31) in DK. For this paragraph see especially B 6, 17, 26, 28, 30, 35; A 28, 29 (Plato, *Soph.* 242d), 37 (Arist., *Metaph.* 985a21 ff.).

19. For evidence that the present age is that of the growing ascendancy of Strife, see *e.g.* A 42 (Arist., *De caelo* 301a15). But it is especially strongly borne out by the actual fragments of the religious poem, in which Love and Strife appear in the human sphere as moral forces, good and bad respectively. The sinless age is in the past, and our history is one of steady degeneration.

For a particular example of an organic substance (bone) formed from a mixture of the elements in certain proportions, see B 96.

20. B 17 init. (line 3 δοιὴ δὲ θνητῶν γένεσις δοιὴ δ᾽ ἀπόλειψις), B 62, A 72 (Aëtius), a 70 (Aëtius). One may observe a remarkable similarity between the language of philosophic poetry in the early 5th century and the

cold prose of Aristotelian science by comparing the life-producing action of κρινόμενον πῦρ in Empedocles B 62 line 1 with that of ἀποκεκριμένη θερμότης in Arist. *Meteorol.* 379b6–8 (quoted in n. 15 above).

How much Empedocles really understood about sexuality in plants is perhaps doubtful. *Cf.* Dr W. H. S. Jones in the *Camb. Anc. Hist.*, vii, 289, writing on Theophrastus:

> That dates are fertilized was known to the Greeks from early times, and Theophrastus describes the process at some length, comparing it to the caprification of figs. The true sexual nature of plants, however, was not yet known. Species, plants and flowers have sex ascribed to them, but generally in a metaphorical sense, 'male' being equivalent to 'barren' and 'female' to 'fertile'.

21. B 57, B 61. For chance as the arbiter of evolution *cf.* B 59 ταῦτά τε συμπίπτεσκον ὅπη συνέκυρσεν ἕκαστα.

Natural selection: Arist., *Phys.* 198b29; Simpl., *Phys.* 371.33 (B 61). G. Rudberg, *Empedocles and Evolution* (Eranos, 1952), warns against going too far in reading back modern concepts into Empedocles.

The double-faced and bisexual denizens of the early world of Empedocles find a parallel in the comic account given by Aristophanes in Plato's *Symposium* 189 d ff. Lucretius agrees that this kind of monster was produced by nature at an early stage, with all sorts of malformed and imperfect creatures (5.837–54); but in spite of his admiration for the *carmina divini pectoris* of his predecessor, he could not allow that animals of different species could ever have been combined (5. 878–924). The lines

> Sed neque Centauri fuerunt, nec tempore in ullo
> esse queunt duplici natura et corpore bino
> ex alienigenis membris compacta

must surely be aimed at Empedocles as well as at the mythologists of early days.

For approaches in ancient Chinese thought to the ideas of evolution and natural selection, see Needham, *Science and Civilisation in China*, vol. 2, 1956, pp. 78–80 (Chuang Tzu 369–286 B.C., i.e. a contemporary of Epicurus).

3. BODY AND SOUL: THE KINSHIP OF NATURE

1. Sherrington, *Man on his Nature* (Pelican ed.) 239, 246, 81–7.

2. Aristotle, *Metaph.* 985b20.

3. *Phys.* 203b6 (DK 12 A 15). In spite of what Professor Vlastos has written (*Philos. Quart.*, 1952, 113), it is much more likely than not that Anaximander called the Unlimited divine. See rather Jaeger, *Theology of the Early Greek Philosophers*, 1947, 29 ff. Vlastos's two arguments against it are both *ex silentio*, and neither is conclusive. He says that τὸ θεῖον does not occur as a substantive for divinity in any Greek text prior to Aeschylus and Herodotus, and that it is one of Aristotle's favourite terms. Apart from the fact that Aristotle, even if paraphrasing, might be correctly conveying Anaximander's meaning, we must consider that we have scarcely any fragments of the actual writing of any 6th-century philosopher, and that the frequency of article plus neuter adjective in a substantival phrase at an early stage is undoubted. Moreover it is only a 'favourite' expression of Aristotle's because his subject is so frequently theology. If Herodotus had been writing a theological treatise, it would doubtless have occurred with more frequency in his work also. Vlastos's second argument again goes beyond the evidence, as denials based on fragmentary sources are bound to do. His main point is of course true, that Anaximander's first principle had nothing to do with the gods or cults of popular religion.

4. For evidence, see DK 13. Anaximenes has been criticized for associating warmth with rarity and cold with density. Cornford (*Principium Sapientiae*, 1952, p. 6) says that if he had ever set a jar full of water outside his door on a frosty night and found it split in the morning, he would have known better. This is scarcely just. As a general rule, bodies (including water) do expand as they are heated and contract as they cool. But for some reason, water, contracting until it reaches a temperature of 39°F. (4°C.), then as it becomes colder and passes freezing point begins to expand again. This exception to the universal rule is still unexplained. We can hardly blame the philosopher if, having hit upon a practically universal truth, he failed to spot the single exception which has hitherto baffled the efforts of scientists to relate it to a general law. Had he made the experiment, and revised his general conclusion in the light of it, it could only have misled him.

5. For fuller treatment, see Guthrie, *Greeks and their Gods*, 1950/54, 138–

141. The passage from Aristotle is *De an.* 410b28. For wind-impregnation *cf.* Homer, *Il.* 16.150 (the father of Achilles's horses was 'the wind Zephyrus') and Vergil, *Georg.* 3.271 ff. For belief in the wind-soul outside Greece, *cf.* Ezekiel, ch. 37 (the valley of dry bones), especially v. 9: 'Come from the four winds, O breath, and breathe upon these slain, that they may live.' An interesting local variant of the Deucalion and Prometheus myths is recorded from Iconium in Lycaonia (*Etym. Magn. S.V.* Ἰκόνιον). In the flood at the time of Deucalion all mankind perished, and when the earth was dry again Zeus ordered Prometheus and Athena to mould figures out of clay and to blow the winds into them and bring them to life.

6. Anaximenes A 10 (Cicero, Aëtius, Augustine), B 2. For the Pythagoreans see especially Aristotle, *Phys.* 213b22 (DK 58 B 30).

7. Arist. *De an.* 411a7 (DK 11 A 22).

8. Diogenes of Apollonia B 4 and 5, A 19 (DK, p. 56, line 3); Aristophanes, *Clouds*, 224–30.

9. The fifth element, usually (and of course rightly) associated with Aristotle, may have been first explicitly recognized by Pythagorean contemporaries of Socrates and Plato, Philolaus and Archytas. See Philolaus fr. 12 and Philoponus *De aetern. mundi* 522.20 Rabe: τὸ πέμπτον σῶμα τὸ ὑπ' Ἀριστοτέλους καὶ Ἀρχύτου εἰσαγόμενον. But these passages, especially the first mentioned, have been the subject of much controversy, which is bound up with the wider and interminable dispute over the genuineness of the fragments of Philolaus. Ross accepts the doctrine for Philolaus (*Arist. Metaph.*, vol. i, p. 138 at bottom). There is at least good evidence that it was recognized by Plato towards the end of his life (Xenocrates *ap.* Simpl. *Phys.* 1165.33).

Anaxagoras identified *aither* with fire, Arist. *De caelo* 270b24 (A 73), 302b4; called the sun an incandescent stone Xenophon *Mem.* 4.7.7. (A 73), Hippol. *Ref.* 1.8.6 (A 42), Diog. L. 2.8 (A 1), etc.

There is considerable truth in Rostagni's remark (*Verbo di Pitagora* 58 n. 1; I translate): 'In fact the περιέχον and the ἄπειρον of Anaximander, the ἀήρ of Anaximenes, the ἄπειρον πνεῦμα of the Pythagoreans etc., were fundamentally one and the same thing: that which sooner or later was called the fifth element'.

10. *Aither* the home of Zeus, Homer, *Il.* 2.412, of the gods in general, Eur. *Bacch.* 393, etc.; identified with Zeus, Eur. fr. 877. Potidaea epitaph,

I.G. i. 442, B.M. *Guide to Sel. Gk. and Lat. Inscriptions*, 1921, no. 9. See also Eur. *Suppl.* 533 f., fr. 971, *Hel.* 1014–16. (The matter of this and the preceding paragraph is somewhat more fully treated in *Greeks and their Gods* 38, 207 ff., 262 ff., 323 f.) One should also compare Eur. fr. 839. 8 ff., which was probably written under the influence of Anaxagoras (DK 59 A 112; *cf.* esp. Anaxagoras B 17):

And they go back, what grew from the earth to earth, but what sprang from aetherial seed returns to the vault of heaven. Nothing dies of what is born, but being sundered one from rhe other they display a different form.

11. Heraclitus, B 30, B 118. *Cf.* B 36 ('It is death to souls to become water'), B 77, B 117. Arist. *De an.* 405a24 (A 15). Aristotle and the Peripatetics recognized two sorts of exhalation, a moist and a dry (*Meteorol.* 341b6). Philoponus's words are (*De an.* 87.11) πῦρ δὲ λέγει οὐ τὴν φλόγα ... ἀλλὰ πῦρ λέγει τὴν ξηρὰν ἀναθυμίασιν· ἐκ ταύτης οὖν εἶναι καὶ τὴν ψυχήν.

12. Plato, *Phaedo* 81 c.

13. Origin of the stars, A 42 (Hippol.), A 71 (Aët.).

14. Mind outside the mixture, B 12 *init*. In B 11 he says: 'In everything there is a portion of everything, except Mind; and some things contain Mind also.' The things in question are *living* things (Arist. *De an.* 404b1 ff.). These Mind 'controls' in a special sense (B 12, ii. 38 line 4 DK), by entering into and animating them. It becomes in fact their soul (ψυχή Arist. *De an.* 405a13 ἔοικε μὲν ἕτερον λέγειν ψυχὴν τε καὶ νοῦν ... χρῆται δ'ἀμφοῖν ὡς μίᾳ φύσει κτλ.). But it still remains distinct from all forms of body, even *aither*, and no inconsistency is involved, other than a purely verbal one. Überweg-Praechter rightly say (12th ed., p. 101): 'Rein und unvermischt ist nur der Geist, was natürlich nicht hindert, dass in manchem anderen Geist enthalten ist.'

Plato's complaint, *Phaedo* 98 b; Aristotle's, *Metaph.* 985a18. Mind starts the motion, Anaxagoras B 12; then withdraws, B 13.

15. The original chaos, in which 'nothing was plain on account of smallness', is described in B 1 and 4, the rotation (περιχώρησις) and its effect in B 12. No birth or perishing, but only mingling and separation, B 17. To elucidate the whole of Anaxagoras's theory of matter is beyond the scope of these (and perhaps of any) lectures, but those willing to face its obscurities

I

may be referred to the discussions of Cornford, *Class. Quart.*, 1930, 14 ff. and 83 ff.; Peck, *Class. Quart.*, 1926, 57 ff.; Vlastos, *Philos. Quart.*, 1950, 31 ff.; Raven, *Class. Quart.*, 1954, 123 ff.

16. Empedocles B 8, Anaxagoras B 10, A 46 (ii, 18, line 43 DK), A 43 (Arist. *De caelo* 302a18).

17. This paragraph depends chiefly on B 1, B 2, B 4 and B 10.

18. Plato, *Apol.* 26d. Almost all our quotations from Anaxagoras are supplied by Simplicius. Unfortunately he has only quoted from that part of the work which deals with first principles and cosmogony, and our information on the rest of its contents is indirect.

The biological points are from Arist. *Gen. An.* 736b30 (A 107) and *De respir.* 470b30 (A115). On the origin of life see Diog. L. 2.9 (A 1) ζῷα γίγνεσθαι ἐξ ὑγροῦ καὶ θερμοῦ καὶ γεώδους, ὕστερον δὲ ἐξ ἀλλήλων, and Theophr. *Hist. Plant.* 3.1.4 (A 117) Ἀ. μὲν τὸν ἀέρα πάντων φάσκων ἔχειν σπέρματα καὶ ταῦτα συγκαταφερόμενα τῷ ὕδατι γεννᾶν τὰ ζῷα. (Cf. *Caus. Plant.* 1.5.2.)

19. Irenaeus *Contra haeres.* 2.14.2 (A 113). A plant is a ζῷον ἔγγειον, Plutarch, *Quaest. Phys.* 1.911 D (A 116). For Plato's similar view see *Tim.* 77c. The soul ἀερώδης, Aët. 4.3.1 (A 93; the Plutarchean version has here οἱ ἀπὸ Ἀναξαγόρου. See Diels, *Dox.* 387). Relation of Anaxagoras to Anaximenes, compare B 1 and Theophr. *De sensu* 59 (A 70: rare and thin = hot, dense and thick = cold; *aither* is thinner and hotter *aer*).

20. Sherrington *o.c.* 180. Speaking to the British Association in 1956, Dr W. H. Thorpe, F.R.S., said that 'undoubtedly some apparent lines of demarcation between man and animal nature had become blurred'. 'He thought it was the conclusion of many and various disciplines that the world of living things appeared now as far more of a unity than was conceivable 100 years ago'. (*Times* report, 31 Aug. 1956.)

21. The kinship of human and animal life is a necessary presupposition to the doctrine of transmigration, which is attested for Pythagoras by his contemporary Xenophanes (*Xenoph.* B 7). One may also quote Porphyry's life of Pythagoras. Neoplatonic sources must of course be used with the greatest caution, but apart from the fact that his informant may have been Aristotle's pupil Dicaearchus, who is mentioned by name some sixteen lines earlier (see Rohde, *Rhein. Mus.* 1872, 26 f.; Wehrli however omits this passage from the

relevant fragment of Dicaearchus), his language here is reassuring. It shows unusual caution, and a real effort to confine himself for once to what he may regard as certain. Of course we read him in the light of Xenophanes's testimony and the existence of the same complex of beliefs in Empedocles in the early 5th century. What Porphyry says is (V.P. 19, DK 14.8a, vol. i, 100, line 36):

> What he said to his disciples no man can tell for certain, since they preserved such an exceptional silence. However, the following facts in particular became universally known: first, that he held the soul to be immortal, next that it migrates into other kinds of animal, further that past events repeat themselves in a cyclic process and nothing is new in an absolute sense, and finally that one must regard all living things as kindred (ὁμογενῆ). These are the beliefs which Pythagoras is said to have been the first to introduce into Greece.

The magical side of Pythagoreanism appears especially in the *acusmata*, adopted, though doubtless not originated, by the Pythagoreans. These were a series of injunctions like 'to spit on one's nail-parings and hair-trimmings', 'to rub out the mark of a pot in the ashes' (also of one's body in the bed), 'not to wear a ring', etc. On these see M. P. Nilsson, *Gesch. Gr. Religion*, i, 665–9.

22. Empedocles believed that everything, plants as well as animals, had consciousness and even the power of thought, an opinion which Sextus Empiricus found 'surprising' (παράδοξον), but which he was able to confirm from a line of Empedocles's own poem (B 110, line 10). For transmigration of the soul into a shrub, as well as into a bird or a fish, see Emped. B 117. He condemns flesh-eating on the grounds of transmigration in B 137, and forbids the eating of laurel leaves B 140. Quoting this passage, a speaker in Plutarch (*Quaest. Conv.* 3.1.2, 646 D) argues that it is wrong to pluck the leaves of any tree, since the tree feels pain. (The laurel was the 'king of plants', for Empedocles said that the best lodging for a human soul was among animals a lion, and among plants a laurel. See B 127.)

Abstinence from flesh among the Pythagoreans is vouched for by Eudoxus (DK 14.9, vol. i, p. 109, line 6), Onesicritus (a Cynic contemporary of Alexander the Great cited by Strabo, DK *ib.*, line 10, where for 'Kalanos' read 'Onesikritos'), and the jibes of the Middle Comedy (DK 58 E, i, pp. 478–80). Some authorities, including Aristotle, said that it was confined to certain species (DK 58 C 3 and B 1 *fin.*, p. 451: the latter passage is assigned to Aristotle by Ross, Oxf. Trans., vol. xii, p. 138, but the attribution does not seem clear from the context. See also 58 C 4, p. 464, line 38), or to certain parts of animals (58 C 6, p. 466, line 11). There was also a determined attempt on the part of some to deny prohibition altogether. This seems to be traceable to Aristoxenus in the 4th century. See Gellius, *Noct. Att.* 4, ch. 11 (partly quoted in DK 14.9, i, p. 101), Diog. L. 8.20 (DK *ib.*) and 12, Porph. V.P. 15. The denial is opposed by Iamblichus, V.P. 25.

For the Pythagorean distinction between life and soul see Alex. Polyhist. *ap.* Diog. L. 8.28 (DK, i, p. 449, line 24).

23. For the relation between the nature of things and the shape of their atoms in Democritus, see Theophr. *De sensu* 61 ff. (DK, ii, pp. 117 ff.). For a description of soul-atoms and their relation to fire, Arist. *De an.* 405a5 ff., etc. (DK A, 101 ff.). Superiority of soul to body as its tenement (σκῆνος), B 37 and 187. Soul of a kind even in dead bodies, A 117 (Aët.).

It is interesting to compare a passage in Plato's *Philebus* where the relationship of 'the fire in us' to the pure fire in the heavens is described just as it might have been by an earlier philosopher, but it is made clear that this like the other elements is only a part of our bodies. The soul is now something entirely incorporeal. In Plato's physiology, fire played an important part in sensation, for sight was made possible by fire (i.e. light) from within us streaming out and coalescing with the fire (light) outside. (See *Tim.* 45b ff.) But for him this is only one of the instruments *through* which the soul operates, not, as a Presocratic would have said, the perceiving soul itself. What Socrates says in the *Philebus* is (29b ff.):

Each of these (i.e. the material constituents of our bodies) in us is small and inferior and in no way pure, and its potency is not worthy of its true nature. Consider them all in a single example. There is fire in us, and fire in the whole. The fire in us is small and weak and inferior, but the fire in the whole is marvellous in its bulk and in its beauty and in all the potency that belongs to fire. Now does the universal fire have its origin and its nurture and its growth from the fire in us, or on the contrary do mine and yours and that of other living creatures get theirs from that other fire?' (He and his interlocutor agree that the first alternative is inconceivable.) 'Yes, you would say the same about the earth in animals and that in the whole world, and all the other elements that I asked you about a little earlier'. (So they agree that our whole body in all its constituents is dependent on the same constituents in the universe outside.) 'Further, we say that our own bodies have a soul, and whence could they have got it, if it were not that the body of the universe is besouled, since it has constituents the same as ours and even better?'

24. Iohannes Catrares (14th cent.) in his dialogue *Hermippus*, quoted by DK as Democritus B 5 (no. 2, vol. i, p. 136, line 46). For this work see note higher on same page of DK.

25. Dr J. W. S. Pringle, F.R.S. (from an unpublished broadcast on *The Origin of Life*, delivered in 1956).

26. It is however of some interest that the question of the biological reality of species is again under lively discussion today, and the outlook seems to have changed considerably since forty or fifty years ago. A textbook on scientific method in its 1924 edition declared: 'The fixity of species in the organic world is, in fact, now entirely discredited' (F. W. Westaway, *Scientific Method*, p. 129). But to take a single example, Dr G. S. Carter, in the *British Journal for the Philosophy of Science* for May 1952, assails the view that owing to their evolutionary origin, the concept of species is necessarily a vague one incapable of being accurately defined. He says:

> That certainly was Darwin's view, it was the general view until the latter part of the 19th century, and indeed until twenty or thirty years ago. But opinion is now different, and I think the majority of systematists would say that the species, at least in zoology, is an objective fact of nature that can be defined as clearly as other biological concepts. . . . The older view neglected the facts that on any theory of evolution interbreeding is necessary for the production of intermediate forms, and that interbreeding does not normally occur in nature between forms that have reached the species level of differentiation, though occasional hybrids may be found.

The question seems to be to some extent one of definition (What is 'the species level of differentiation'?), and no doubt different opinions will continue to be expressed.

4. CYCLES OF EXISTENCE: THE GOLDEN AGE

For a full documentary treatment of the subjects touched on in this and the next lecture, see A. O. Lovejoy and G. Boas, *Primitivism and Related Ideas in Antiquity*, Baltimore (Johns Hopkins Press), 1935. It seemed best not to consult this work until the lectures were written.

1. See Diog. Laert., *prooem.* 3, quoted above, ch. 1, n. vii. For the analogy between seasonal and historical cycles, with the example of the Pythagoreans, see Eudemus *ap.* Simpl., *Phys.*, p. 732, Diels, and compare the idea of the Great Winter in Aristotle (quoted on p. 65 above). The Greek theory of the detailed repetition of history is echoed by Vergil in the fourth Eclogue (lines 34 ff.):

> Alter erit tum Tiphys et altera quae vehat Argo
> Delectos heroas; erunt etiam altera bella
> Atque iterum ad Troiam magnus mittetur Achilles.

For the general popular picture of time as moving in a circle rather than a straight line, *cf.* Aristotle, *Phys.* 223b13 ff., and Cornford's remarks thereon in *Plato's Cosmology* (1937), 103 f. It had of course been adopted by the Stoics, in whose system it was fundamental, being bound up with the notion of a Great Year, and also with the more specifically Stoic idea of a cosmic conflagration. See von Arnim, *Stoic. Vet. Frr.*, i, 109 (p. 32) and ii, 623 ff. (pp. 189–91).

The poem quoted is Horace, *Odes* 4.7, in A. E. Housman's translation.

2. Great Year in Plato, *Tim.* 39d, on which see Cornford, *Plato's Cosmology* (1937), 116 f.; W. Koster, *Mythe de Platon, de Zarathustra et des Chaldéens* (1951), 55 ff. In general see Heath, *Aristarchus*, index s.v. Great Year; Taylor, *Timaeus* 216–9; B. L. van der Waerden in *Hermes*. 1952, 129 ff.; Ch. Mugler, *Devenir Cyclique et Pluralité des Mondes* (1953), 68 f. (See also M.'s index: in general the conclusions of this book must be received with caution; see review in *Class Rev.*, 1955, 46–8).

The Great Winter in Aristotle, *Meteorol.* 352a28 ff.

3. Diod. 1.6.3. *Cf.* Censorinus *De die nat.* 4, quoted by Wehrli, *Dikaiarchos* (*Schule des Arist.*, Heft 1, 1944), p. 22.

4. Polybius 6.5, in Sir Ernest Barker's translation (*From Alexander to Constantine*, 1956, 108). *Cf.* Lucr. 5.338 ff., Arist. *Politics* 1269a4.

5. Plato, *Tim.* 22b ff., *Critias* 109d–e.

6. *Laws* 676a ff. In a later book, at 781e, he apparently leaves open the question whether the human race had no temporal beginning at all, or has simply existed for a very long time.

7. For Aristotle and the Flood see pp. 25–6 and ch. 1, n. 17 above. The passages concerning the repeated loss and discovery of philosophy and the arts are fr. 13 Rose (Oxf. Trans. vol. 12, p. 80), *Metaph.* 1074b10, *Meteorol.* 339b27. *Cf.* also *De caelo* 270b19, *Pol.* 1329b25. We may add Philoponus in *Nicom. Isag.* 1.1, if all that Ross prints as being from Aristotle (O. Tr. 80–1) is indeed his.

8. The Latin texts in question are perhaps too well known to need citation. See Horace *Odes* 4.2, 33–40, Verg. *Aen.* 6.791–4. There is also of course the famous Fourth Eclogue, whoever may have been its subject. Tacitus too, as a natural corollary to his attacks on the moral degeneracy of his own age, accepted without question the superiority in this respect of the men of the remotest past: 'Vetustissimi mortalium, nulla adhuc mala libidine, sine probro, scelere, eoque sine poena aut coercitionibus agebant' (*Ann.* 3.26). Parallels in ancient Chinese thought to the two contrasting views of primitive society may be found in vol. 2 of Dr Needham's *Science and Civilisation in China*. The idea of peaceful simplicity is represented by the Taoists (p. 106), and that of primitive man as having been, until the introduction of law and order, savage and quarrelsome, by the Mohists (166 f.). But on the evidence provided by Needham the Taoist account seems somewhat vitiated by its obvious hostility to the Confucians.

9. R. Reitzenstein (*Stud. zum antiken Syncretismus, Studien Warburg* 7, Leipzig, 1926, 57 ff.) suggested that the succession of ages symbolized by metals is Oriental, probably Iranian, in origin. *Cf.* F. Dornseiff, [*Hesiods*] *Werke und Tage und das alte Morgenland* (1954, repr. in *Kl. Schr.* I, 1956, p. 73, n. 4), and see also Prof. H. C. Baldry's article *Who Invented the Golden Age?*, in *Class. Quart.* 1952, 83–92. Baldry, who mentions the Oriental traditions on p. 85, contends that Hesiod was the first Greek writer to use the symbolism of gold in describing a happier existence in the past. His article contains much information on the history of the whole conception. J. Gwyn Griffiths (*Archaeology and Hesiod's Five Ages, Journal of the History of Ideas*, 1956, pp. 109–19) upholds the thesis of a historical basis for Hesiod's scheme. The myth of the ages is found in *Works and Days*, 109 ff., where Hesiod introduces

it as 'another story' of the decline of the human race from happiness, after telling first the story of Pandora's box. For the myth of the metals in Plato, see *Rep.* 415a ff.

10. Hesiod, *Works and Days*, 42 ff., Lucr. 2.1150–2, 1164–74. It is perhaps of some interest that the phrase 'spatio defessa vetusto', used to describe 'all things' in line 1174, is the same that Lucretius applies to the earth herself when like a woman she gets past the time of bearing (5.827).

11. Plato, *Laws* 713c ff. and *Politicus* 271c ff.
It may be noted that the idealization of rural life which was a natural consequence of urban growth led later to a portrayal of the age of Kronos or Saturn as an age of farming. (Hesiod knew too much about the realities of a farmer's life to idealize its labours.) So Aratus and some Roman writers, though in Vergil *Georg.* 1.125 we still read that 'ante Iovem nulli subigerunt arva coloni'. See E. Graf *Ad aureae aetatis fabulam symbola* (*Leipziger Stud. z. Class. Philol.* 8, 1885), p. 55. Graf is however rather too ready to see a deliberate description of the Golden Age in any sentimental glance at the past as better than the present.

12. For the ironical use of 'golden' we have for instance the following from Ovid's description of the Age of Iron (*Met.* i, 137):

> Nec tantum segetes alimentaque debita dives
> Poscebatur humus, set itum est in viscera terrae,
> Quasque recondiderat Stygiisque admoverat umbris
> Effodiuntur opes, irritamenta malorum.
> Iamque nocens ferrum ferroque nocentius aurum
> Prodierat.

Other examples will be found in Baldry (see n. 9), 86 f.
Rivers of gold, etc., in Lucr. 5.911:

> Aurea tum dicat per terras flumina vulgo
> Fluxisse et gemmis florere arbusta.

On exceptions to the generally agreed simplicity of the 'Golden Age', see Baldry 86, and for Aristophanes's jokes about 'Kronian' characteristics, *ib.* 84. These latter, it should be admitted, may be typical only of the attitude of Athenians in the late 5th century, not of the Greek mind in general.

13. Emped. B. 128 (Porph. *De abst.* 2.21, 27). For the continuous production of leaves and fruit by the trees, see B 77–78, reconstructed from a comparison of Theophr. *Caus. plant.* 1.13.2 with Plut. *Qu. Conv.* 649c. DK

assign this to the π.φύσεως because it seems probable that E. provided a physical explanation, but it may belong to the καθαρμοί. See DK *ad loc.*

Records of Mycenaean times provide some evidence that offerings to the gods were in fact mostly bloodless in that 'golden age' nearly a thousand years before Empedocles. So Ventris and Chadwick, *Documents in Mycenaean Greek* (1956), p. 128: 'The usual offerings are grain and flour, oil, wine, figs and honey, occasionally wool.' (The tablets, on pp. 199 ff., are actually from Knossos.)

14. *De abst.* 4.2 ff. (Wehrli, *Dikaiarchos* 1944, fr. 49). The arguments by which E. Graf tried to explain away the references to abstention from meat, as being Porphyry's distortions of Dicaearchus, are not very convincing. (*o.c.* n. xi, pp. 45-8).

15. It is not however by any means certain that Hesiod himself intended to limit his Golden Race to a meatless diet. See E. Graf, *o.c.* p. 13.

16. Lucr. 5. 206-12. As we see a little later on, Lucretius was not quite consistent in this, just as the traditions on which he drew were not consistent. Vergil on the other hand speaks of this perversity of nature as a new feature, only evinced when the age of Saturn had already been replaced by that of Jove (*Georg.* 1.150 ff.).

17. In China the Taoists also condemned metallurgy as a source of evil (Needham, *Science and Civilisation in China*, vol. 2, 1956, p. 108).

18. As in so many other things, Epicurus was here following Democritus. See Democritus B 284. But all that we know of Epicurus leads us to believe that he had made it his own by the proof of experience.

19. Lucr. 5. 942-4, 925-30, 988-1009. Bailey comments that in his account of primitive life Lucretius follows Diodorus closely. This accords with his general view that the passage in Diodorus is Epicurean in origin. In fact both Diodorus and Lucretius were probably making their choice from among a variety of traditions some of which were much older then Epicurus. Although to a considerable extent the two accounts tally, we notice the following differences: (i) There is no mention in Diodorus of primitive man being stronger and better able to withstand the hardships of life, as well as less susceptible to disease (Lucr. 990). (ii) Diodorus makes no suggestion that fruits were 'plurima etiam maiora'. (iii) Lucretius says:

> Nec commune bonum poterant spectare neque ullis
> Moribus inter se scibant nec legibus uti.

This is not quite in accordance with Diodorus's statement that even at this early stage, and purely as a defence against wild beasts ἀλλήλοις βοηθεῖν ὑπὸ τοῦ συμφέροντος διδασκομένους, ἀθροιζομένους δὲ διὰ τὸν φόβον, ἐπιγιγνώσκειν ἐκ τοῦ κατὰ μικρὸν τοὺς ἀλλήλων τύπους. (This passage is not quoted by Bailey in his comparison.)

20. Diod. 1.8. 1–2, 5–6.

21. Soph. O.C. 1224–8, Theognis 425–8, Arist. fr. 44 Rose (Oxf. Trans., vol. 12, p. 18).

22. Plato, *Politicus* 269c ff.

23. Soph. *Antigone* 365–8.

5. THE IDEA OF PROGRESS

1. M. Finley, *The World of Odysseus*, revised ed., London, 1956, 111 f. Homer, *Od.* 9. 106–15, 272–6, 125–7. The absence of ships and seafaring is one of the many facts which could, according to the temperament of the writer, be fitted into either a 'Golden Age' or a 'progressive' scheme of the history of culture. For Hesiod it characterized the Golden Age (*Erga* 236), as also for the Stoic Aratus (*Phaen.* 111), and among the Roman poets Virgil (*Georg.* 1.136), Ovid (*Met.* 1.96), and others. In Aeschylus on the other hand (P.V. 467 f.) it was a mark of the primitive misery and helplessness from which Prometheus rescued mankind.

2. Plato, *Laws* 680b (*cf.* Aristotle, *Eth. Nic.* 1180a28, *Pol.* 1252b23) and 681e (quoting *Il.* 216–8). According to a passage of Philoponus which Ross includes among the fragments of Aristotle (*in Nicom. Isag.* 1.1, Aristotle Oxf. Tr., vol. xii, p. 81), the reason why they 'still dwelt on the slopes' was that memories of the Flood made them afraid to dwell on the plains. Compare Plato's comment at 682b.

3. On 'Golden Age' touches in Homer, see E. Graf, *Ad aureae aetatis fabulam symbola* (*Leipz. Stud. z. Class. Philol.* 8, 1885), pp. 4–6. With οἷοι νῦν βροτοί εἰσιν compare the remarks of Nestor at *Il.* 1.260–8.

4. Xenoph. B. 18. See the discussion on this by W. J. Verdenius and J. H. Loenen in *Mnemos*. 1955, p. 221 and 1956, 135–6. The fire which Prometheus stole for men διδάσκαλος τέχνης πάσης βροτοῖς πέφυκε καὶ μέγας πόρος (110 f.).

5. P.V. 85 f. ψευδωνύμως σε δαίμονες προμηθέα
καλοῦσιν, αὐτὸν γάρ σε δεῖ προμηθέως.

The common form for the abstract noun is of course προμήθεια, and the formation of προμηθεύς suggests a person, 'the fore-thinking one'. But it seems more natural that Kratos should refer to the Titan's lack of foresight as such, and Aeschylus could as easily have written, without any loss in the play on words αὐτὸν ὡς προμηθείας σε δεῖ (or even, since he was no stickler for caesura, simply αὐτὸν γὰρ κτλ). At Pind. *Ol.* 7.44 προμαθέος αἰδώς it looks as if the word is intended as a noun both common and abstract. (Schroeder and Bowra print both words with small initial letters.) If the surface meaning is, however, 'Aidos daughter of Prometheus', the significance of the name is at least being emphasized in a fully conscious act of personification. It occurs again as a common noun (I think for the only other time in a text of the classical period) in the Medicean ms. of Aesch. *Suppl.* 700, where editors have followed Hermann in emending to προμαθίς.

The lines referred to in the last sentence of the para. in the text are 443–4:

ὡς σφας νηπίους ὄντας τὸ πρὶν
ἔννους ἔθηκα καὶ φρενῶν ἐπηβόλους.

For another play on the meaning of the name Prometheus see Plato, *Prot.* 361d.

A different etymology has been suggested for the name, deriving it from Sanskrit *pramanthas*, a fire-stick. Even if this should be etymologically correct, it is obvious that the Greeks in the 5th century had no inkling of it. (See Lovejoy and Boas, *Primitivism and Related Ideas in Antiquity*, 1935, p. 200.)

6. Soph. *Ant.* 332 ff. The *Antigone* was probably produced in 441. Aeschylus died in 456, and the P.V. was probably one of his latest plays. The progressive scheme of civilization is outlined yet again by Theseus in the *Supplices* of Euripides (195 ff.), with the mention of language, housing, navigation and commerce, and omen-reading. All this κατασκευὴ βίῳ is said to be the gift of a god, but as with Prometheus in Aeschylus, the first thing he bestowed was σύνεσις, intelligence (line 203). We need not credit Euripides with a more religious outlook than Sophocles (*pace* Uxkull-Gyllenband, *Griech. Kultur-Entstehungslehre*, Berlin, 1924, 23 ff.).

7. Anaxagoras B 21b, Democr. B 154, Protag. B 1 and 4. On Anaxagoras in this connexion Uxkull-Gyllenband is interesting, though he perhaps sees more in our meagre texts than most scholars would be prepared to (o.c. n. 6 above, 10 ff.).

Modern scholars have tied themselves into knots trying to discover all the possible, and some impossible, meanings to be attributed to Protagoras's dictum πάντων χρημάτων μέτρον ἐστιν ἄνθρωπος. There is no sufficient reason to doubt that Plato and Aristotle understood it correctly, and they both explain it with admirable clarity (Plato *Theaet.* 152a, Ar. *Metaph.* 1062b12). Indeed as Lewis Campbell pointed out in his edition of the *Theaetetus* (1883, p. xxix), Plato's almost verbatim repetition of the explanation in *Theaetetus* and *Cratylus* makes it more than likely that it too is an actual quotation from Protagoras himself.

8. *Prot.* 320c ff. There is no need to recapitulate here the discussion that has taken place through the years over the question how far the myth is a genuine work of Protagoras. References for it will be found in M. Untersteiner, *The Sophists* (trans. Freeman, Oxford, 1954), p. 72, n. 24. The style is certainly not Plato's. It is self-consciously poetic, not naturally so as in Plato's own myths, and displays also a rhetorical balance of phrase such as the Sophists loved to display. No doubt Plato could imitate their style, but as Adam says, it is not a caricature such as one might expect if Plato were writing a mere parody. In substance, though cast in mythical form, it is a serious statement of an evolutionary view of human society, parts of which can be paralleled in earlier Ionian thought, while some features seem to be original. There seems every reason to ascribe such a theory to Protagoras, and since his views must have been well known, the idea that Plato put it all together himself and then made the Sophist utter it seems a little far-fetched. Moreover, Plato has taken such pains to characterize the speakers in the *Protagoras*, which is perhaps the most vividly dramatic of all his dialogues, that it is scarcely conceivable that he should not also put into their mouths the most characteristic of their doctrines. (So Morrison in C.Q. 1941, p. 7.) We are fairly safe in thinking of this as an authentic representation of Protagoras's views, most probably as he expounded them in the work περὶ τῆς ἐν ἀρχῇ καταστάσεως which he is known to have written.

9. See especially the passage quoted on p. 95 above. For our present purpose, it is not necessary to go deeply into the troubled question of sources. I do not wish to 'credit Protagoras with the prehistory in Diodorus', a proceeding which Professor Vlastos deprecates. He is unlikely to have been as

original a thinker in cosmogony and zoogony as he was in other spheres, and even in what he says about the origins of culture he may have made a synthesis of theories that were already abroad in his time. Still less am I pronouncing an opinion on the general question, so much discussed, of the date and authorship of the ideas reproduced in Diodorus. On these see J. S. Morrison in C.Q. 1941, p. 9, n. 1, and G. Vlastos, *On the Prehistory in Diodorus* (A.J.Ph. 1946, 51–9), where further references will be found. It is hardly controversial to say that, by whatever intermediaries it reached Diodorus, there is in his account material of the 5th century B.C., some of which may be credited to Democritus, the younger contemporary and fellow-citizen of Protagoras, while some is probably earlier.

10. διὰ τὴν τοῦ θεοῦ συγγένειαν (322a). Adam and Croiset follow other editors in ejecting this phrase. The reference, says Adam (*Platonis Protagoras*, Cambridge, 1921, p. 112), can only be to the statement at the beginning of the myth that men were created by the gods and so are to be regarded as their children, but since the beasts were also divinely created, this should apply to them also. More probably, however, no such definite reference is intended. The kinship of men with gods is mentioned as something which does not call for explanation, since it was so universal an article of Greek belief from Homer onwards. *Cf.* for example Hes. *Works* 108 ὡς ὁμόθεν γεγάασι θεοὶ θνητοί τ᾽ ἄνθρωποι, or Pind. *Nem.* 6.1 ἓν ἀνδρῶν, ἓν θεῶν γένος, ἐκ μιᾶς δὲ πνέομεν ματρὸς ἀμφότεροι· διείργει δὲ πᾶσα κεκριμένα δύναμις . . . ἀλλά τι προσφέρομεν ἔμπαν ἢ μέγαν νόον ἤτοι φύσιν ἀθανάτοις. Alex. Polyhistor *ap.* Diog. Laert. 8.27 quotes as a Pythagorean belief ἀνθρώπων εἶναι πρὸς θεοὺς συγγένειαν κατὰ τὸ μετέχειν ἄνθρωπον θερμοῦ.

But the accepted ground of the belief (not necessarily inconsistent with this one) was man's possession of λόγος or νοῦς, the power of rational thought. This not only raised him above the beasts, but was a faculty that he shared with the gods and hence a proof that he was basically of their kin, though no doubt very much of a poor relation. This was the idea which was carried to philosophical heights in the ὁμοίωσις θεῷ of Plato and ἐφ᾽ ὅσον ἐνδέχεται ἀθανατίζειν of Aristotle. In Homer of course the kinship of men with gods was a much more literal and physical one, but the two conceptions could well exist side by side, some inclining more to the one and some to the other, according as their natures ran to simple piety or religious belief of a more philosophic and rational type.

Adam's minor objection, that the singular τοῦ θεοῦ is 'inaccurate', is of no great weight. Plato uses ὁ θεός and οἱ θεοί more or less indifferently, and it is quite possible for the singular to have a collective sense.

11. So W. Nestle in his edition of the *Protagoras* (Leipzig, 1931), introd., p. 19. Protagoras would then have been in a similar position (albeit rather a curious one) to Frederic Harrison in the 19th century: 'He regarded all religions as false, but insisted on the human necessity of worship.' (A. W. Brown, *The Metaphysical Society* (Columbia U.P., 1947), p. 126.)

12. G. B. Kerferd, *Protagoras's Doctrine of Justice and Virtue*, J.H.S., 1953, pp. 42–5. This article deals admirably with some common misconceptions of Protagoras's speech.

13. Those who wish to do so will find an admirable guide in the book of T. A. Sinclair, *Greek Political Thought* (London, 1951).

14. Aristotle, *Metaph.* 997b35 (DK, ii, p. 266), *cf. De an.* 403a12. E. Frank (*Plato u.d. sogennanten Pythagoreer*, 1923, 351), with unnecessary ingenuity, doubted whether Protagoras ever said this, and was more inclined to attribute it to Democritus. Heath on the other hand (*Greek Mathematics*, 1921, vol. i, p. 179) suggested that it was *against* such attacks on geometry that Democritus wrote his treatise περὶ ψαύσιος κύκλου.

6. WHAT IS MAN? THE PHILOSOPHICAL IMPLICATIONS

1. Critias fr. 25 DK ἄτακτος καὶ θηριώδης; Diod. 1.8.1, the first men lived ἐν ἀτάκτῳ καὶ θηριώδει βίῳ; Mosch. fr. 6 Nauck θηρσὶν διαίτας εἶχον ἐμφερεῖς βροτοί; Eur. *Suppl.* 201 f. ὃς ἡμῖν βίοτον ἐκ πεφυρμένου καὶ θηριώδους θεῶν διεσταθμήσατο. Also Lucr. 5. 931.

Most modern researchers would probably say that the 'echo' in these words is an echo of Democritus. It is widely held that this philosopher was responsible for the replacement of the idea of a Golden Age by that of a primitive state of brutishness and misery. From many possible passages one may quote Pohlenz, *Die Stoa* (1948), p. 235: 'Dem romantischen Traum von einem goldenen Zeitalter hatte Demokrit das Bild eines tierähnlichen Urzustandes entgegengestellt, aus dem der Mensch sich erst allmählich emporgearbeitet habe, indem er unter dem Zwange der Not seine geistigen Fähigkeiten entwickelte.' But the 'tierähnlicher Zustand' is already present in Aeschylus, nor are the 'geistige Fähigkeiten' lacking. (To improve their status men must first become ἔννους καὶ φρενῶν ἐπηβόλους.)

Cannibalism: Mosch. fr. 6.14 f., Diod. 1.14.1, 1.90.1, Orph. fr. 292 Kern. Also Cic. *De inv.* 1.2, etc. That men do not eat one another, as some other animals do, was attributed by Hesiod to the gift of δίκη, which, as in the myth of Protagoras, Zeus bestowed on mankind alone. (*Erga*, 276 ff.)

That time alone brought the arts was more emphatically stated by the comic poet Philemon (Meineke, CGF, iv, 54):

> ὅσαι τέχναι γεγόνασι, ταύτας, ὦ Λάχης,
> πάσας ἐδίδαξεν ὁ χρόνος, οὐχ ὁ διδάσκαλος.

2. *Vet. Med.* 3 and 7. Contrast the opinion of Dicaearchus, p. 75 above.

3. For Aeschylus and Protagoras see pp. 82 and 86 above. Add Xen. *Mem.* 4.3.7, *Hymn. Hom.* 20 (Hephaestus), *Vet. Med.* 7.

4. Isocr. *Paneg.* 28; Cf. Xen. *Hell.* 6.3.6. See also ch. 1, n. 18 above.

5. Virg. *Aen.* viii. 314 ff., Diod. 5.66.4. A combination of the Golden Age with a progressive theory of culture seems to have been attempted by Posidonius, though there is no evidence that he posited a yet earlier age of savagery. See Uxkull-Gyllenband, Gr. *Kultur-Entstehungslehren* (1924), pp. 44–6.

6. Eur. fr. 910 Nauck. *Cf.* especially fr. 783, and also other passages cited in the index of DK *s.v.* Euripides (ii. 600 f., entries referring to section 59).

7. P. 67 above.

8. θεασαίμεθα λόγῳ 369a.

9. K. von Fritz, *The Theory of the Mixed Constitution in Antiquity: a critical analysis of Polybius's political ideas* (Columbia, 1954), ch. 3. In Polybius's account of the genesis of a state (6.5.4 ff.), men are brought together by ἀσθένεια, and form a herd under the strongest and boldest, just like animals (ζωηδόν). Contrast Aristotle, *Pol.* i. 1253a7 διότι δὲ πολιτικὸν ζῷον ὁ ἄνθρωπος πάσης μελίττης καὶ παντὸς ἀγελαίου ζῴου μᾶλλον, δῆλον.

10. See Aristotle, *Eth. Nic.* i. 1097b 5–21 and *Pol.* i. 1252b 28–1253a 18. The only Greeks bold enough to suggest that the individual was αὐτάρκης

in himself, and community life superfluous, seem to have been the Cynics. See Miss A. N. M. Rich's paper *The Cynic Conception of* αὐτάρκεια, *Mnemos.* 1956, pp. 23–9.

11. Shorey, *Recent Interpretations of the Timaeus*, Cl. Phil. 1928, pp. 343 f.

12. See especially *Epinomis* 982c–d. Dr S. Sambursky rightly attributes the change in outlook to the invention of machines and machine-produced artefacts as opposed to the products of handicraft: 'We of the machine age have grown accustomed to an entirely different association of ideas. The essence of every machine is that it repeats the same movement exactly; so that we use the expression 'automatic' to indicate precisely a movement that is devoid of reason, a 'soulless' movement. But in the age of arts and handicrafts, the exact reproduction of a model or form was regarded as a sign of the artist's divine inspiration.' (*The Physical World of the Greeks*, London, 1956, p. 54.)

13. A more immediate source was probably Ovid. *Cf. Met.* 1.19: *Frigida pugnabant calidis, umentia siccis.* Spenser could have read this either in the original or in Golding's translation, which appeared in 1567. The Hymn to Love, from which the quotation is taken, was written in 1595–6.

THE MESSENGER LECTURES

In its original form this book consisted of six lectures delivered at Cornell University in April, 1957, namely, the Messenger Lectures on the Evolution of Civilization. That series was founded and its title prescribed by Hiram J. Messenger, B.Litt., Ph.D., of Hartford, Connecticut, who directed in his will that a portion of his estate be given to Cornell University and used to provide annually a 'course or courses of lectures on the evolution of civilization, for the special purpose of raising the moral standard of our political, business, and social life'. The lectureship was established in 1923.

Index